BIRMINGHAM
– BUSES –
AT WORK
1942-69

2489 (JOJ 489)

The 64 bus terminus at Erdington was positioned opposite the old 2 route tram terminus after the trams had been replaced on Saturday 4 July 1953. Some of the buses that replaced the trams were a batch of 'New Look'-front Crossleys, drafted in to Miller Street garage. Exactly 50 years later, on 4 July 2003, one of the buses of the same class, the preserved Crossley DD42/6 2489 (JOJ 489) commemorates the half-centenary by recreating the first journey of the replacement 64 route, which was actually undertaken by a Crossley, though from a different batch. *Author*

BIRMINGHAM
– BUSES –
AT WORK

PART 2: WARTIME PROBLEMS, A NEW FLEET AND ENGINES AT THE REAR, 1942-1969

David Harvey

FORWARD

· THE NOSTALGIA OF BRITAIN ·
from
The NOSTALGIA Collection

First published in 2006

British Library Cataloguing in Publication Data

A catalogue record for this book is available from the British Library.

ISBN 1 85794 262 0
ISBN 978 1 85794 262 0

Silver Link Publishing Ltd
The Trundle
Ringstead Road
Great Addington
Kettering
Northants NN14 4BW

Tel/Fax: 01536 330588
email: sales@nostalgiacollection.com
Website: www.nostalgiacollection.com

Printed and bound in Great Britain

ACKNOWLEDGEMENTS

This book would not have been possible without the many photographers whose work is credited within the text. Most of the photographs came from my own archive, but special thanks are due to Peter Drake of the Local Studies Department of the Birmingham Central Reference Library, who allowed me access to its photographic archive, and to the Kithead Trust, whose archive material was invaluable. I would like to thank my wife, Diana, for her proof-reading skills and grammatical expertise, to Barry Ware, who stoically week after week received, read and corrected another batch of proofs, and to Derek Potter, whose advice about historical and vehicle details is always illuminating and helpful. Finally, thanks to Peter Townsend of Silver Link who agreed to publish these two volumes, and to Will Adams and Mick Sanders, who had the job of squeezing a quart into a pint pot when laying out the book.

BIBLIOGRAPHY

The PSV Circle publications about Birmingham City Transport, PD9 and 10, were vital sources of information, as were the BCT vehicle record cards held at the Kithead Trust in Droitwich Spa. The book *Birmingham City Transport* by Malcolm Keeley et al, published by TPC, as well as the two volumes of *Birmingham Corporation* by Paul Collins were most useful research documents. The news cuttings files held in the Birmingham Central Reference Library and the Transport Committee notes were also extremely helpful.

CONTENTS

ABBREVIATIONS

AEC	Associated Equipment Co	CMS	Commercial Motor Show
ACV	Associated Commercial Vehicles	ECW	Eastern Coach Works
b	built	es	entered service
BaMMOT	Birmingham and Midland Museum of Transport	LNWR	London & North Western Railway
		MCCW	Metropolitan-Cammell Carriage & Wagon (Co)
BCT(&OD)	Birmingham Corporation Tramways (& Omnibus Dept)/ Transport	MCW	Metro-Cammell-Weymann
		MoS	Ministry of Supply
BET	British Electric Traction	MoWT	Ministry of War Transport
BMMO	Birmingham & Midland Motor Omnibus (Co)	MR	Midland Railway
		OMO	One Man Operation
BRCW	Birmingham Railway Carriage & Wagon (Co)	w	withdrawn
		WMPTE	West Midlands Passenger Transport Executive
BTC	British Transport Commission		
CBT	City of Birmingham Tramways Co		

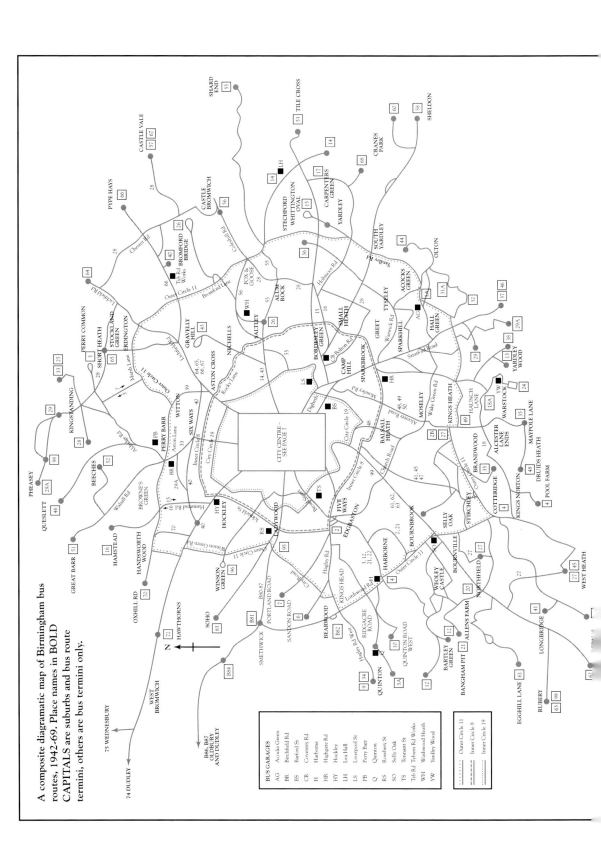

A composite diagramatic map of Birmingham bus routes, 1942-69. Place names in BOLD CAPITALS are suburbs and bus route termini, others are bus termini only.

BUS GARAGES

AG   Acocks Green
BR   Birchfield Rd
BS   Burford St
CR   Coventry Rd
H   Harborne
HR   Highgate Rd
HY   Hockley
LH   Lea Hall
LS   Liverpool St
PB   Perry Barr
Q   Quinton
RS   Rosebery St
SO   Selly Oak
TS   Tennant St
Tyb Rd Tyburn Rd Works
WH   Washwood Heath
YW   Yardley Wood

.... Outer Circle 11
– – – – – Inner Circle 8
·············· Inner Circle 19

This is the second of two books looking at *Birmingham Buses at Work*. The aim of these volumes is to take the reader on an historical journey through time and space, historically and geographically, around the City of Birmingham. Because of the nature of the available material and the types of operation on which the buses were employed, these two volumes show the individual classes of vehicles as they chronologically entered service, as well as depicting the buses throughout their working lives.

This second book starts with the first deliveries of the first buses built to the new Ministry of War Transport's specifications for Birmingham City Transport in September 1942 and finishes with the delivery in September 1969 of the first buses

of the last order ever placed by the Corporation. The aim of the book is to look at Birmingham buses actually on the road, showing the development of the Birmingham motor bus during the abandonment years of the tram and trolleybus systems, and to show the changes in bus design from when the vehicles were front-engined, half-cab vehicles, which passengers boarded by way of an open back platform, until they were rear-engined, front-entrance, one-man-operated, state-of-the-art buses.

All of this was done under the auspices of the Transport Department of Birmingham City Council. During the municipal operation of public transport, Birmingham only ever had four General Managers: Alfred Baker from 1903 to 1928, his son Arthur Chantry Baker from 1928 until his death 'in harness' in 1950, W. H. Smith from 1950 until 1962, and finally W. G. Copestake who became the PTE's first Director of Operations in October 1969. There was a continuity of operations and development that, if at times a little conservative as regards its vehicle purchasing, was innovative regarding ticketing, timetabling and operation. There was a tradition of a quality product going on the road to serve the citizens of Birmingham, so the bus fleet was always spotlessly presented in the dignified dark blue and primrose cream. A bus was never seen with a dented panel, and a broken-down bus was so rare an occurrence that it drew crowds to watch the catastrophe. Up until the last journeys into the garages on 30 September 1969, the Corporation buses had worked for the people of Birmingham. Throughout 65 years of transport operation, the Corporation had an aura of civic pride that, as far as the buses were concerned, lasted from 1914 until 1969. This book captures *Birmingham Buses at Work* in different periods of time, contrasting locations and different operating conditions, but always 'looking immaculate'!

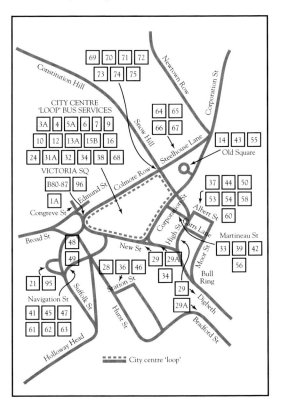

City contrasts

1915 (HOV 915)

The 68 service was introduced on 12 November 1967 and followed the 17 route to Garretts Green Lane before going via Sheldon Heath Road to the island at The Radleys. It went around the City 'Loop' with one of its major pick-up points being in Victoria Square outside the Canadian Pacific Railway's information centre and the Joe Lyons Tea House. Just three months after the service began, 1915 (HOV 915), a nearly 19-year-old, exposed-radiator Daimler CVG6 with a Metro-Cammell body, stands waiting to pick up passengers. The surviving members of these solidly built buses would only operate on the new 68 service for a maximum of 11 months before all the class were withdrawn. 1915 still looks in fine condition, but within weeks, at the end of April 1968, it would be withdrawn from service. *J. Carroll*

2103 (JOJ 103)

Two of the few inter-suburban bus services that were not the domain of single-deckers were the 40 and 40A, which were successors to the 5 tram route introduced on 1 October 1950. The 40A was the peak-time extension to the Dunlop tyre factory in Holly Lane from Gravelly Hill, where 2103 (JOJ 103), a Daimler CVD6 with a 'New Look' front and a Metro-Cammell H30/24R body, is waiting at the Bundy Clock. This bus entered service in 1951 and lasted until September 1966. Behind it is the penultimate BCT 'Standard' bus, 3226 (MOF 226), a Crossley-bodied Daimler CVG6, working on the 65 route from Short Heath; unlike 2103, it has yet to have its front wings cut back in order to get more air to the brakes. It is hard to imagine that about ten years earlier Gravelly Hill was the three-way junction where the last three tram routes met, and even harder to believe that ten years after 2103 drew away from this stop and went on its way to Villa Road, Lozells, this area would be subsumed beneath the Gravelly Hill Interchange, where the M6 and A38M meet. *A. B. Cross*

1.
1942–1946
STRUGGLES THROUGH THE WAR

Throughout the inter-war period both Birmingham and Coventry had developed as main centres of the motor trade. Not only did Birmingham's vehicle manufacturers and their component suppliers adapt to make military vehicles, but their car assembly plants could also be easily converted to make aircraft and aero-engines. In addition, after 1936, the Government financed the construction of four new 'shadow' factories in the Birmingham area to build military materiel, military engines, armament and aircraft fuselages. The sheer scale of wartime manufacturing in the city is almost beyond belief, and on reading the following it is not surprising that Birmingham City Transport's resources of buses, trams and trolleybuses were stretched almost to breaking point as they took war workers into the factories from pick-up points all over the city for each shift, which normally occurred three or four times a day.

The Rover Organisation managed the factories at Acocks Green and Lode Lane, Solihull, while Austin's aircraft factory was built adjacent to the Longbridge factory at Cofton Hackett. During the war the Austin Aero Company manufactured more than 2,700 aircraft, including more than 1,500 Fairey Battle light bombers and the four-engined Short Stirlings and Avro Lancaster bombers as well as Horsa gliders, while the car works produced more than 120,000 military vehicles from 8hp military cars to 3-ton trucks, including 13,000 of the famous K2 ambulance that were nicknamed 'Screamers'. Morris-Commercial was responsible for the third and largest 'shadow' factory at Castle Bromwich, just off Chester Road, which covered some 345 acres. Castle Bromwich made around 300 Avro Lancasters and just over 11,000 Supermarine Spitfires, which accounted for nearly two-thirds of all Spitfire production! In addition, Morris-

Commercial produced its famous 4x4 field artillery tractors, 3-ton trucks and Morris M 10hp light utility vehicles and Crusader tanks, while Wolseley made full-track personnel carriers and millions of fuses as well as anti-personnel mines, until the Ward End factory literally blew up after being bombed in 1941. Latterly, Wolseley made more than 1,800 Horsa glider wings for the D Day invasion and around 135,000 depth charges. Serck Radiators Ltd in Greet made all the radiators and air coolers for Rolls-Royce Merlin engines, while SU Carburettors also supplied carburettors and fuel-feed products for the same aero-engine. Joseph Lucas made more than 20,000 electro-hydraulic gun turrets for bombers as well as electrical components and searchlights. Lucas also carried out a lot of the development work on the combustion and fuel systems on the Welland and the later Derwent turbo-jet engines for the Gloster Meteor, which was the first Allied operational jet fighter. The list goes on, with MCCW making more than 4,000 tanks, while BSA in Small Heath produced every sort of gun imaginable as well as military motorcycles. Ariel Motors in Selly Oak, James in Greet, Norton in Aston and Velocette in Hall Green also manufactured motorcycles. ICI's Kynochs Works in Witton made 67 types of shells and cartridges, and Dunlop at Fort Dunlop made tyres and wheels for aircraft as well as for nearly every type of military road vehicle. Meanwhile, down in the pastoral haven of Cadburys chocolate factory, the company set up Bournville Utilities Ltd to manufacture rockets, respirators and aircraft parts. Even the back-street jewellers in the Jewellery Quarter of Hockley were turned over to making precision parts of radar equipment.

The mass evacuation of children began on 1 September 1939, which inevitably put an extra strain on the bus resources as they shuttled children between their collection points and the railway stations. By March 1941, as the bombing reached its worst, the number of children evacuated had reached nearly 40,000.

Between August 1940 and April 1941 there were very few nights when there were not bombs dropped somewhere in the city. There were 77 enemy raids on Birmingham, with more than 2,000 people being killed and around 1,100 public buildings, factories, offices and shops destroyed. On the night of 19-20 November 1940 some 350 bombers raided the city, causing the death or injury of 1,353 people, including a direct hit on the BSA factory in Armoury Road, which killed 53 workers. Water resources had become so low, even in the canals, that the Birmingham Fire Brigade later admitted that if the bombers had returned within 48 hours, any fires would just have to be allowed to burn. This was the first night a bus was badly damaged when 814 (BOP 814) was blown over in Queen Street alongside Highgate Road garage, where every bus in the garage lost all its window glass. On 22-23 November Hockley garage was bombed, with 88 buses damaged, six partly burned out and 17 totally burned. On 11-12 December 1940 the longest air-raid of 13 hours took place, while on 9-10 April 1941 came the last big air-raid on Birmingham. During the raid some 650 high-explosive bombs rained down on the city and 1,121 citizens were either killed or injured; afterwards no tram could reach either its outer or inner terminus on any route. This raid destroyed much of the Bull Ring, High Street and the Prince of Wales Theatre in Broad Street.

During this desperate period, in the months after the Battle of Britain, the availability of buses was very poor. Birmingham City Transport was allocated a total of 149 new buses, which was a surprisingly small number in view of the huge numbers of works services operated by the Corporation's fleet. Yet by as early as September 1942 the number of women employed in the city had risen by 150% in three years, while the whole of Birmingham's workforce had gone up by more than 65%, with more than 400,000 people being employed in manufacturing military materiel.

Not including the eight 'unfrozen' buses delivered by the summer of 1942, the Corporation was able to put into service a total of three Daimler CWG5s, six Guy 'Arabs', 78 Guy 'Arab' IIs, 55 Daimler CWA6s, and seven Daimler CWD6s. These were delivered between the autumn of 1942 and February 1946, with standard Ministry of War Transport-designed composite bodies being received from Park Royal, Weymann, Brush, Duple and Strachan. The six Daimler CWD6s that entered service in June 1945 were among the first of the type to be manufactured. A batch of metal-framed Northern Counties bodies was allocated by the Ministry of War Transport, but these were rejected and it is believed that they were transferred to Coventry City Transport. In addition 50 of the piano-fronted AEC 'Regents' were rebodied by Brush between 1943 and 1944, while in response to the MoWT instruction of June 1943, the 33 service to Kingstanding was turned over to producer-gas operation. This involved the conversion of 23 petrol-engined AEC 'Regent' 661s, which were operated, albeit very slowly, in 1943 and 1944.

As early as 25 September 1939, just three weeks after the outbreak of the Second World War, 17 bus routes were cut back from their outer termini or in some cases discontinued. Although the introduction of the 10 service to Quinton Road West occurred on 19 May 1940, most service alterations involved reductions in frequency, which also curtailed some further routes from their pre-war suburban termini. In addition to the sudden closure of the highly profitable Nechells trolleybus route on 30 September 1940, there was a general diminution of availability of buses, while the requirements of factories on war work increased almost week on week. The darkest day of the war as far as bus services was concerned was 21 February 1943 when 19 bus routes were subjected to further suburban cut backs after 9pm, which continued until 16 October 1944, while all cross-city services and routes using the one-way City loop were suspended after 7.30pm, a situation that remained until 25 June 1945. These measures, which reduced the operation by around 40,000 miles each week, were designed to save fuel and slow down tyre wear.

In Birmingham the MoS-bodied wartime buses had a particularly short life, with one being in service for only 41 months before it was withdrawn. A briefly considered idea was to have the Daimler CWA6s rebodied in about 1949, as they had the 'easy-change' Wilson pre-selector gearbox, but this idea was quickly dropped on the grounds of cost, and as a result new post-war chassis were ordered and the Daimlers were all withdrawn before their second major overhaul. The last buses of this type, significantly Daimlers, were withdrawn at the end of January 1951.

By the end of the war the reckoning up had to be done. During the hostilities BCT had lost 41 trams and 20 buses, 111 employees with HM Forces had been killed, 6,000 vehicle windows had been blown out, and one of the two trolleybus routes had been suspended, but the trams were still running on 21 routes. The tram system had been due to close in 1944, with the conversion of Washwood Heath's routes, but the outbreak of the war had halted this. It was obvious that the trams would need to be replaced

and even the instigation of a major rebuilding exercise of the earlier eight-wheeled trams proposed for 1948 would only keep the fleet running for a few more years. Similarly a large quantity of the pre-war bus fleet stock was getting near to the end of its economic life and was due for replacement. This was at a time when delivery dates for new vehicles were being measured in years rather than months, and orders were being placed more with a view to get an order in a queue for distant delivery than for the expectation of imminent arrival!

One 'new' bus came into service and pointed the way towards the new post-war standards. This was a 1939 Daimler COG5, 1235 (FOF 235), which had received a new Brush body and re-entered service on 1 May 1946.

Despite all these pressures on the bus fleet, All-Night bus services on an hourly basis began on 15 April 1946 along 17 main roads leading from the All-Night termini in either Bull Street outside Greys store or in Colmore Row alongside St Philip's Churchyard.

2239 (JOJ 239)
The use of single-deckers in Birmingham was limited, but they were used intensively, being employed on numerous routes that had height restrictions with canal aqueducts or railway bridges. In 1950 30 Leyland 'Tiger' PS2/1s were purchased to replace almost immediately the 45 worn-out pre-war Daimler single-deckers. The new Leylands were both attractive and powerful vehicles, capable of turns of speed that many a contemporary local coach operator could only dream of. They were bought mainly for use on the Northfield-Cotteridge-West Heath 23 route and for the private hire and special work that the City Transport Department provided for the Education Department. As roads were lowered beneath low bridges, several routes

such as the 2B were lost to double-decker operation, resulting in the new single-deckers becoming under-used, especially at garages such as Hockley and Liverpool Street. To get more use from them, particularly in the morning peak periods, they would turn out on double-decker services. That is the situation here, as one of Perry Barr garage's 'Tigers', 2239

(JOJ 239), displays the dreaded 'SERVICE EXTRA' destination as it works on the 5 route. It is turning into Colmore Circus from Snow Hill Ringway in about 1966, with the massive Snow Hill station still dominating the city skyline. The 5 service was normally operated by double-deck buses, so this was a case of 'the biter being bit'! *A. J. Douglas*

1332-1337 (FOP 332-337)
Guy 'Arab'; Gardner 5LW 7.0-litre engine; Weymann MoS H30/26R body; allocated by MoS 3.1942, es. 9.1942-11.1942, w 6.1948-10.1949

This model was built by Guy Motors as a replacement for the Leyland 'Titan' TD8 wartime bus, which was cancelled when Leyland Motors had its production facilities turned over to military vehicles. The first tranche of wartime 'Arabs' numbered 500 were easily identifiable as they usually had straight, short, front wings, whereas the later model, known as the Mark II, had curved front wings. They were fitted with a four-speed constant-mesh gearbox. All the buses were delivered in an all-over grey livery, brown rexine-covered seats in both saloons, and unglazed rear emergency windows in the upper saloon.

1334 (FOP 334)
It is a measure of how evasive these buses were that the best photograph of one of the batch of six actually at work was taken after the sale of the vehicles. This class of bus had the distinction of being the first vehicles built to the MoWT's specifications to be allocated to the Corporation. They were sent to Yardley Wood garage, still fairly new since its opening in 1938, during the autumn of 1942, where they operated on the two Yardley Wood services, 13 and 24, as well as the long suburban 18 service. In more or less original condition, 1334 (FOP 334) is being operated by Davies of Merthyr Tydfil, who managed to get well over seven years' service out of it, albeit having strengthened the bulkheads and fitting D-shaped end windows in the lower saloon. The former 1334 waits in Merthyr before going on service to Cefn-Coed. *D. A. Jones*

1336 (FOP 336)
The only known photographs of these camera-shy Guy 'Arabs' in Birmingham livery are two taken of 1336 (FOP 336) after its withdrawal in October 1949, in the yard of W. T. Bird. It is awaiting sale, early in 1951, with its glory days long behind it. Despite being only seven years old, 1336 looks a particularly worn-out bus having been repainted only once. It was not operated as a bus again, being sold to a showman who cut off the top-deck and converted it to a lorry. The bus stands alongside 195 (EOG 195), an 11-year-old BRCW-bodied Daimler COG5 that was in such a poor condition that it never found a buyer and was cut up by Birds not long after 1336 was sold. *R. A. Mills*

1338-1340 (FOP 338-340)
Daimler CWG5; Gardner
5LW 7.0-litre engine;
Duple MoS H30/26R body;
allocated by MoS 11.1942,
es 3.1943, w 1.1949-5.1950

Being the largest operator of the pre-war Daimler COG5 model, it was surprising that of the 100 CWG5 chassis built, Birmingham was only allocated these three vehicles. The CWG5 model was a COG5 but without the use of alloy steels, thus making the chassis heavier. The model had a Wilson pre-selector gearbox and a fluid flywheel. The Duple bodies had the shell-backed rear dome and could be recognised as one of the quite early bodies built at Hendon as the bottom of the driver's door and off-side cab window were at the same level as those in the lower saloon. Later the design was modified and these two off-side windows were raised by several inches.

1339 (FOP 339)

The bus is turning across Old Square in front of Lewis's department store and the pedestrianised Minories, which enabled shoppers to walk between the two blocks of the shop on a strange surface of rubber blocks. The Minories was also a favourite spot for suicide attempts, while another depressing fact of life was the 'greyness' of wartime Britain. Even some of the new buses were grey, including 1339 (FOP 339), which entered service on 18 March 1943. Although it was fitted with brown rexine-covered seats, the gloom of the rear of the upper saloon can be explained by the lack of glazing in the rear emergency window. Initially operated from Yardley Wood garage, 1339 is working on the 14 service to Glebe Farm, being operated at that time by Liverpool Street garage. It is also displaying a slipboard for Kitts Green, which was about a mile beyond the usual Kitts Green terminus, and a destination only used on a limited number of journeys. Just to the front of the bus is an Austin Ruby Seven, parked at the entrance to Upper Priory. *C. F. Klapper*

1341-1358 (FOP 341-358)
Guy 'Arab' II; Gardner
5LW 7.0-litre engine;
Weymann MoS H30/26R
body; allocated by MoS
5.1943, es 10.1943-3.1944,
w 1.1949-5.1950

These were the first of the 'Arab' II model to be delivered and could be distinguished from their predecessors by their curved front wings. The Weymann bodies were the same as those on the 1332-1337 batch, except that there was no opening ventilator in the lower-saloon nearside front window overlooking the bonnet. Nos 1341-1354 were painted grey and all were equipped with wooden seats until the first overhaul.

1342 (FOP 342)

Standing in Lonsdale Road at the rear of Harborne garage is 1342 (FOP 342), waiting for its next duty in about 1948 with the anonymous and ambiguous 'SPECIAL' destination display. The Guy 'Arab' II chassis could be distinguished from the wartime 'Arab' by having a radiator about 4½in further forward to ensure that a Gardner 6LW engine could be fitted. This meant that all 'Arab' IIs were 26ft 4½in long, too long for the current Construction & Use Regulations, which had to be relaxed in order for them to operate. The Weymann body was an attractive design, though it lacked curvature to the upper-deck front profile. The late-Victorian bay-windowed terraces disappearing into the distance date from the last years of the 1890s, when the site of the future Harborne bus garage on the opposite side of the road was a large timber yard. *E. Chitham*

1350 (FOP 350)

Below Most of the first batch of Weymann-bodied Guy 'Arab' IIs were delivered in an all-over grey livery. On a rainy day soon after entering service on 1 January 1944, 1350 (FOP 350), still in its original grey livery, waits at the Bundy Clock in Hawthorn Road, Kingstanding, when working on the 28 route. The bus is carrying a slip board on the radiator showing that it is travelling towards the city terminus in Station Street. Because of the difficulties that drivers experienced with the reverse-gated constant mesh gearbox, during their brief careers with BCT many of the Guy 'Arabs' were used in their latter days as driver training

vehicles. This bus, typical of BCT's wartime stock, was only repainted once, in September 1946, emerging from Tyburn Road Works in full fleet livery on 6 October 1946, and amassed only 142,000 miles in service before being withdrawn at the end of January 1950. On the opposite side of Hawthorn Road is the row of shops including, strangely, Baker's the butchers! These 1930s premises had two-storey flats above the shops, which contrasted with the surrounding council houses. *Author's collection*

1353 (FOP 353)

Bottom Harborne garage had a number of Guy 'Arab' IIs allocated to its vehicle complement largely to take over, albeit briefly, from the AOB-and AOG-registered Daimler COG5s of 1934 and 1935. Standing at the rear entrance to the garage in 1949, facing Lonsdale Road, is a pair of Weymann-bodied buses, though they are from different batches. The bus on the left is 1353 (FOP 353), which entered service on 11 January 1944, while on the right is 1376 (FOP 376), a member of the 1366-1377 batch of similarly Weymann-bodied Guy 'Arab' IIs. By this time the tiny artillery-style headlights, made by Butlers of Small Heath, had been replaced with full-sized ones, a process that seemed to be undertaken with a greater frequency on the Corporation's Guys than on the comparable Daimler CWA6 vehicles. *E. Chitham*

1359-1365 (FOP 359-365)
Daimler CWA6; AEC A173 7.58-litre engine; Duple MoS H30/26R body; allocated by MoS 9.1943, es 1.1944-3.1944, w 1.1949-11.1950

This batch were all painted grey and were equipped with wooden seats until the first overhaul. The CWA6 model replaced the Gardner-engined CWG5 by having the slightly more powerful and certainly smoother-running AEC six-cylinder engine, coupled to a Wilson pre-selector gearbox and a fluid flywheel. This produced a somewhat more sophisticated vehicle than the contemporary Guy 'Arab' and was obviously more favoured by the Corporation, whose pre-war aim was to have an 'easy-change' gearbox fleet of buses.

1359 (FOP 359)

Right Still fitted with the artillery-style small headlights and a black-painted radiator, 1359 (FOP 359) is on the 43 service to Nechells in Aston Street in about 1947, passing the row of shops built below the fire officers' flats that were part of the brick-and-Portland-stone-faced Central Fire Station complex styled to look like a Georgian mansion and opened in 1935. The 43 route had been the 7 trolleybus service, 'temporarily' taken out of use at the end of September 1940 as the arcing of the skate placed in the track on journeys between Washwood Heath tram depot and Bloomsbury Street was a threat to the blackout, especially around the Tame Valley industrial establishments. The overhead wiring was gradually dismantled over the next three years so that inevitably the trolleybuses were never re-instated, though the remains of some of the overhead is still visible. The Nechells trolleybus service had an allocation of 16 vehicles, none of which was more than nine years old at the time of the abandonment. 1359 faired little better, having a service life in Birmingham of barely five years before eventually finding its way back into service in October 1951 with the South Western Bus Company of Ceylon, where it ran, eventually as a single-decker, until December 1965! *Commercial postcard*

1365 (FOP 365)

Above right The last of the first batch of Duple-bodied Daimler CWA6s, 1365 (FOP 365), is parked in Washwood Heath depot yard on 22 April 1950. Its destination box shows the old 22 Bolton Road tram replacement route, although by this time it was only used as a shortworking of the long 28 service. The bus had only been back in service for just over a fortnight, having been given an interior repaint at Tyburn Road Works and, judging by its smart exterior, a good sprucing-up of the blue and primrose livery. The Duple bodies always had a cream waistband below the lower saloon windows, and it was here that the Hendon-built bodies scored regarding body strength as there was a double body frame rail beneath the panels that gave a degree of extra strength to the composite construction. 1365 was withdrawn at the end of November 1950 and was subsequently exported to Ceylon. *G. F. Douglas, courtesy of A. D. Packer*

1366-1377 (FOP 366-377)
Guy 'Arab' II; Gardner 5LW 7.0-litre engine; Weymann MoS H30/26R body; allocated by MoS 9.1943, es 11.5.1944-1.9.1944, w 9.1949-11.1950

This batch was the same as the previous batch of Weymann-bodied Guy 'Arab' IIs, but took four months for entry into service to be completed. They were all equipped with wooden seats until their first overhaul.

1371 (FOP 371)

Below Until 1939, all the 'big three' football grounds were served by tramcars. The first trams to go were the West

Bromwich Albion football services on 2 April 1939, when the Handsworth, West Bromwich, Wednesbury and Dudley trams were replaced by buses. The second football ground to lose its trams was St Andrew's, the home of Birmingham City, on 2 October 1948, when the 84 and 90 routes were converted to bus operation. The final football ground to lose its tramcar special services was Villa Park. On Christmas Day Aston Villa lost 1-0 to Newcastle United, and on New Year's Eve tramcar 18, one of the 1-20 class of Aston bogies, closed the 3X route, which went along Witton Lane, alongside Villa Park. It was not until 21 January 1950, when Aston Villa played Middlesbrough, beating them 4-0, that buses were used on the Villa Park football specials for the first time. On that Saturday, when the author was

celebrating his second birthday, 1371 (FOP 371) waits in Witton Lane for the 30,460-strong crowd to leave the ground. The poster in the front upper saloon window shows that the bus will go back to Station Street in the City Centre, then go on to terminate in Selly Oak. *J. Cull*

1373 (FOP 373)

Below The original Snow Hill Station was opened on 1 October 1852 and was drastically rebuilt, work commencing in 1910 and taking two years. Because of the descent of Snow Hill and the narrow area of land available for the station between Snow Hill and Livery Street, the two new island platforms were more than 1,200

feet long, necessitating the enlargement of the viaduct beyond the length of the old station's platforms as far as the Great Charles Street bridge. This created an enormous void below rail level at the junction of Snow Hill and Great Charles Street. The station building here was on three levels and was used for staff accommodation and stores and, at street level, for parcel redistribution and, originally, for stabling the railway's horses. Vehicle access for parcels traffic from Snow Hill was on the right of the parked late-1938-registered Morris Ten Series M. Coming down Snow Hill from the distant Colmore Row and Bull Street junction over the cobbles and the abandoned single outbound

tram tracks in August 1945 is 1373 (FOP 373), working on the 16A service with a slipboard showing that it is going to Hamstead. Opposite the railway station, just to the left of the somewhat battered Hillman Minx car, the evidence of recent wartime bombing is all too evident. *Birmingham Central Reference Library*

1374 (FOP 374)

Top right It is the autumn of 1945, and although the war is over the newly found peace looks a pretty bleak and hollow one. The centre of Birmingham had been severely damaged by bombing raids and has a look of being run down. In the background, overlooked by Edward Grey's furniture and carpet store, is Steelhouse Lane, where the tram stops are visible for the three services to the Erdington area of the city. The patched-up bus shelter outside Snow Hill Station had been put up in the last years of the tram services to Handsworth, West Bromwich, Dudley and Wednesbury, which had been converted for bus use on 2 April 1939. Their old tracks still lead out of Livery Street, but would never be used again. On the right of Colmore Row, occupying the corner of Bull Street, is Boots the Chemist's shop, still with is windows boarded up as replacement glass would have still been difficult to obtain. The site to the right of the Morris Ten series M was still, as locals called them, 'a bomb building' site, which would soon be occupied by a temporary wooden building serving as premises for Boots. Bus 1374 (FOP 374), looking very much like it did two years earlier when it was new, still retaining its wartime grey roof although it has lost is white-edged front wings, barks its way past the Rover Twelve car working towards its terminus alongside St Philip's Churchyard. It is one of Yardley Wood garage's buses and is being employed on the 24 service to Warstock. *Birmingham Central Reference Library*

1375 (FOP 375)

Above right On 4 August 1949 one of Harborne garage's Weymann-bodied Guy 'Arab' IIs, 1375 (FOP 375), has pulled up at Princes Corner, Harborne, on the 3 route. The

bus is parked just beyond the Harborne Park Road junction with the corner of Albert Road, which is just in front of it on the right. Princes Corner, named after Prince Albert, was the destination of the original 1904 Birmingham Motor Express Company's bus service to Harborne. The largest shop in this small block of six retail outlets between is the double frontage of Wrenson's grocery store, Birmingham's leading family grocers, who survived until the advent of large supermarkets. Behind the bus is an Albion 2-ton van. This bus stop was unique in the city as it told the prospective passenger that this was where to catch the bus to 'Queen's Park', in Court Oak Road. The route had been extended to Worlds End Lane as the 3A service on 13 January 1937, so 1373 is on the shortworking to West Boulevard. *E. Chitham*

1378 (FOP 378)
Guy 'Arab' II; Gardner 5LW 7.0-litre engine; Weymann MoS H30/26R body; allocated by MoS 9.1943, es 9.1944, w 12.1950

This bus had a metal-framed, experimental 'bearerless' body (body number M.2671) and had thicker body pillars than normal. In addition it had radiused saloon window-pans. It was equipped with wooden seats until its first overhaul.

1378 (FOP 378)
The bus is waiting alongside the long row of shelters outside St Philip's Cathedral and its tree-lined churchyard in Colmore Row when working on the 6 route to Sandon Road on 28 July 1950. These elaborate shelters, opposite the Grand Hotel, were used by all the bus services that travelled along Colmore Row. After the one-way-street system was introduced on 5 June 1933, all traffic travelled towards Victoria Square before turning in front of the Town Hall and into Paradise Street, or left, around Galloways Corner, and into New Street. 1378 will take the former route on its way towards Broad Street. It was one of the six highbridge Guy 'Arab' IIs that had experimental metal-framed bodies that Weymann was allowed to produce towards the end of 1944, of which Birmingham City Transport had two. As well as the window-pans and radiused corners to the windows, they had cab windows with curved corners that were to be a feature of early post-war Weymann bodies. *J. Cull*

1379 (FOP 379)
Guy 'Arab' II; Gardner 5LW 7.0-litre engine; Park Royal MoS H30/26R body; allocated by MoS 11.1943, es 18.2.1944, w 10.1949

This was the first Park Royal body on a Guy 'Arab' chassis allocated to the Corporation and was actually delivered within three months of being ordered. It was painted grey and had wooden seats until its first overhaul.

1379 (FOP 379)
Without fanfare, rather like its Park Royal MoS predecessor 1327 (the Leyland 'Titan' TD7), the first of the Park Royal-bodied Guy 'Arab' IIs, 1379 (FOP 379), seems not to have been captured on film and is seen here on the Promenade at Dunoon having been sold off by the Corporation in April 1950 to Dunoon Motor Services. Entering service in February 1944, after one repaint back into fleet livery in May 1946, it was taken out of service at the end of September 1949 after amassing only 140,000 miles. It is 20th of a 'flaming' August in 1953 – just look at the weather! – and after three years service with Dunoon, FOP 379 appears not have been altered since its Birmingham days. One can only wonder why the General Manager and the Transport Committee wanted to get rid of the wartime buses with such almost indecent haste; once sold to a dealer such as W. T. Bird of Stratford-upon-Avon, former Birmingham buses were quickly snapped up by independent operators such as Dunoon MS because of their reputation for being well maintained and in good condition. *D. Caton*

**1380-1383 (FOP 380-383)
Guy 'Arab' II; Gardner
5LW 7.0-litre engine;
Weymann MoS H30/26R
body; allocated by MoS
11.1943, es 8.1943-9.1943;
1383 fitted with Brush
MoS H30/21R body from
OG 388 and converted to
dual control trainer 98,
8.1952-1.1968; w 9.1949-
11.1950**

These buses were equipped with
wooden seats until their first overhaul
and were the same as the 1366-1377
batch.

1380 (FOP 380)

Top right Parked on the forecourt of
Selly Oak garage on 14 November
1950, just two weeks before
withdrawal, is Weymann-bodied Guy
'Arab' II 1380 (FOP 380). Parked
alongside it is 1403 (FOP 403),
which, although three months
younger, would be taken out of service
on the last day of 1950. By this time
these were some of the last 'utility'
Guys to remain in passenger service
with Birmingham, but even so were
largely confined to peak-hour extras or
learner duties. The buses at Selly Oak
were housed at the Gibbins Road end
of the premises and the traction poles
for the trams are just visible above the
months-old Weymann-bodied Leyland
'Tiger' PS2/1. On the right is one of
Harborne garage's Daimler CVA6s,
which has just 'popped in for a cup of
tea' before taking its pupil back home.
J. Cull

1383 (FOP 383)

Above right Looking for all the world like a normal wartime
bus, 1383 (FOP 383) stands at the entrance to Quinton
garage in about 1962. Surviving in this condition until
January 1968, FOP 383 would have been a wonderful
vehicle to preserve, but alas it was missed and was despatched
to Harwood Finance in Barnsley in June of the same year.
Perhaps the only clue as to the peculiarity of this vehicle was
that it carried the fleet number 95, from the service vehicle
fleet, rather than its true identity of 1383. Although it was a
standard Guy 'Arab' II it was fitted with a 1943 angle-
staircase Brush MoS-style body, which had replaced the
original Vulcan body on AEC 'Regent' 418. The

combination of Guy 'Arab' II chassis and Brush 'utility'
body never looked a very happy one as all six buses rebuilt in
this way (1383/84/96/1401/33/34) seemed to have the body
rather 'perched' on the chassis. Although they retained a full
complement of thick-cushioned 1930 seats in both saloons
and even bells that 'dringed' rather than making a bell-like
ring, the six buses had been converted to dual-control
trainers. The instructor sat on a raised dais behind the
trainee, rather than alongside as in the case of Midland Red's
dual-control trainers, and had his own steering wheel, which
can just be seen behind the driver's seat. He also had a full
set of all the other controls except the accelerator pedal, so
that if there was an emergency…! *L. Mason*

1384 (FOP 384)
Guy 'Arab' II; Gardner
5LW 7.0-litre engine;
Weymann MoS H30/26R
body; allocated by MoS
11.1943, es 11.1944; 1384
fitted with Brush MoS
H30/24R body from
OG 418 and converted to
dual-control trainer 95, 2.1952-1.1968;
w 12.1950

This bus was the second of the six metal-framed bodies built by Weymann (body number M.2674) to be operated by BCT and had thicker body pillars than normal with radiused saloon window-pans. It was equipped with wooden seats until its first overhaul.

1384 (FOP 384)
Weymann's experimental 'bearerless' metal-framed body gave a more attractive-looking vehicle than the more usual composite bodies produced by this Addlestone-based bodybuilder, which, unlike other manufacturers, barely altered its standard MoS design between 1942 and 1946. 1384 (FOP 384) turns left from Bristol Road South, Longbridge, with the overhead wires for the 71 tram route

disappearing towards Rubery, into the rather unimaginatively named Bristol Road South as it travels towards Northfield. This turn was a good test for the trainee driver as he will have been made to stop at the junction and, as here, is pulling away in first gear before attempting a quick 'snap' change into second gear to get him over the steep rising bridge at Longbridge Station, about 100 yards away. The bus is working on a Learner duty and has the necessary L plate in the downstairs front window, though it would be at least 18 months before it would be rebodied with the wartime Brush body from AEC 'Regent' 418 and converted to a dual-control trainer. Appropriately, as it is passing the Austin Motors Longbridge car factory, it is being followed by a rare early post-war Austin A70 Hampshire, which cost £608 and was only in production between 1948 and 1950. *Author's collection*

1385-1392 (FOP 385-392)
Daimler CWA6; AEC A173 7.58-litre
engine; Park Royal MoS H30/26R body;
allocated by MoS 6.1944 but with Brush
H30/26R body, es 2.1945-3.1945, w 7.1949-
10.1950

The Park Royal bodies were to a 'relaxed' design announced by the MoS in December 1944, although compared to the earlier bodies the rear dome was slightly less severe, with a

curved roofline in the rear dome rather than the 'shell-back' of the first utility designs from this bodybuilder.

1385 (FOP 385)
The first of the batch was 1385 (FOP 385), and despite having an MoS 'relaxed' body design, it was delivered with only a pair of opening half-drop windows in each saloon. It stands on the cobbled section of the road surface in Old Square at the terminus of the Lea Hall routes in 1949 outside the large shop owned by Cranes, Birmingham's premier showroom for pianos. The cobbles were a remnant of the an earlier age, but were kept at places where buses repeatedly stopped as they resisted dents in the surface from standing vehicles. The bus was working on the 14B service, introduced on 21 September 1938 as an extension to Lea Village from Audley Road. Behind it is 1801 (HOV 801), a 1948 Daimler CVD6 with a Metro-Cammell body, which is working on the 43 service to Nechells. *R. Marshall*

1391 (FOP 391)

The 14 route was extended from Lea Village to Tile Cross on 29 May 1949, and on 9 July bus 1391 (FOP 391), its paintwork already looking a little shabby, but sporting a chrome radiator presumably inherited from a withdrawn COG5 via the garage stores, is turning across Upper Priory in Old Square, with the tall Lewis's department store towering above the surrounding streets. Lewis's had opened its new premises in 1929 and would continue to trade until 13 July 1991. Behind the distant bow-collector-carrying 762 class tram, travelling along Corporation Street on either the 8 or 10 route, are the

elaborately arched windows of the large Stork Hotel, which stood on the corner of Lower Priory and was opened in about 1881. To the left of the bus is the island in the middle of Old Square, with its underground gents and ladies lavatories with 'wash and brush-up' facilities. Standing against the wrought-iron railings around the entrance to the conveniences was a flower-seller with her galvanised buckets full of blooms. On the Old Square side of the island was a row of six telephone boxes, and there was often a man who sold hot potatoes and roast chestnuts from a mobile oven on cold winter days. Behind the bus, and looking as if it is coming out from the Minories, which ran between the two halves of Lewis's, is a Ford Anglia EO4A 8hp car, new in 1946. Bus 1391 was withdrawn from service on New Year's Eve 1949. *J. Cull*

1393-1400 (FOP 393-400) Guy 'Arab' II; Gardner 5LW 7.0-litre engine; Park Royal MoS H30/26R body; allocated by MoS 2.1944, es 3.1944-4.1944; 1396 fitted with Brush MoS H30/24R body from OG 416 and converted to dual-control trainer 96, 5.1952; converted to tree-lopper 1.1959-1.1968; w 10.1949-12.1950

These buses had standard Park Royal bodies and were equipped with wooden seats until their first overhaul.

1395 (FOP 395)

The two-tone Wolseley Super Six 25hp, dating from 1937, stands in front of Lewis's department store in Old Square behind virtually new 1395 (FOP 395). It carries a Park Royal H30/26R body, but for the first time on a Guy the body has a deep, cream-painted waistrail, which improved its appearance. Bus 1395 entered service towards the end of March 1944 and later in the same year is still equipped with wartime headlight masks and white edging paint on the bodywork. It was at this time allocated to Liverpool Street garage, and is working on the 43 service, hurriedly introduced on 30 September 1940 to replace the Nechells 7 trolleybus route. As though waiting to be re-energised, above the bus are the trolleybus overhead wires, which would, in fact, never be used again. *C. F. Klapper*

1396 (FOP 396)

Below Looking very smart is Liverpool Street garage's dual-control trainer, BCT service vehicle 96, which was a combination of Guy 'Arab' II 1396 (FOP 396), which entered service in March 1944, and a Brush 'utility' body of September 1943. The body had started life on the 1930-built chassis of 398 (OG 398), but this had been transferred in May 1948 to a previously English Electric-bodied 'Regent', 416 (OG 416), which had been originally converted to a dual-control trainer in August 1938. The bus is standing in Adderley Street some time before January 1959, when it was converted to serve as a tree-lopper by the removal of the top deck. What was unique about the six Guy 'Arab' IIs converted to serve as driver trainers was that, although they remained in service, leading a somewhat twilight existence for nearly 20 years, they never ran as PSVs in this condition. So although the bus is waiting at the City Circle 19 bus stop, it is waiting more in hope than in anger! Behind the bus, parked near to the distant junction with Watery Lane and opposite the United Wire Works factory, is an early Morris-Commercial LD-type van. *R. F. Mack*

1398 (FOP 398)

Bottom The trolleybus wires are still in place in Old Square on 20 June 1945, while two apparently identical wartime buses wait to pick up their passengers. But 'Oh, what a difference a livery makes!' 1398 (FOP 398), a Park Royal-bodied Guy 'Arab' II that entered service from Liverpool Street garage in early April 1944, is about to pull away from the 14 bus stop outside the premises of Crane's Pianos; its destination display is 'GLEBE FARM 14', but it has a slipboard on the radiator showing KITTS GREEN, a service which was extended on 21 September 1938 to serve J. Booth's new non-ferrous metal foundry. 1398 was one of the buses delivered by Park Royal to have a cream-painted waistrail and a thin black livery line below the lower saloon windows. One easy distinguishing feature of the wartime Park Royal body was the neat way in which the tops of the cab windows were at the same level as the top of the windscreen and the bottom of the canopy, as shown on both these buses. Parked behind is 1408 (FOP 408), one of the next batch of Park Royal-bodied Guy 'Arab' IIs, delivered in June and July 1944, which has the more normal style of wartime livery that eliminated the cream waistrail; it is working on the 43 bus route to Nechells. *J. Cull*

1401-1402 (FOP 401-402)
Guy 'Arab' II; Gardner 5LW 7.0-litre engine; Strachan MoS H30/26R body; allocated by MoS 3.1944, es 2.1945-3.1945; 1401 fitted with Brush MoS H30/21R body from SV 57 (OG 414), new 10.1943 on 401 (OG 401), and converted to dual-control trainer 93 from 1.1953 to 1.1968; w 7.1950-12.1950

These were perhaps the most severe-looking of all the wartime bodies delivered to BCT. They looked, from the front, like the current Park Royal design, but from the rear they had a very tall, gaunt appearance. They were equipped with wooden seats until their first overhaul.

1402 (FOP 402)
The Strachan body design was something of a curate's egg. The component parts, such as the front of the upper deck, the cab area and the lining-up of the top of the lower saloon windows with the top of the driver's signalling window in the door, were all neatly done. Unfortunately, the almost vertical rear looked as tall as a block of flats, which combined with an expanse of very deep panelling between the decks to produce a body that just 'didn't look right'. These two buses took about 12 months from allocation by the MoWT to delivery, which made them the last Guy

'Arabs' to be delivered to Birmingham Corporation by between two and three months. 1402 (FOP 402) is standing on Selly Oak garage forecourt alongside Chapel Lane on 16 March 1950, having been used on a driver training duty. This was quite a common practice for the ageing wartime Guy fleet, and 1402 had only another four months left before it was withdrawn from service. It had only done 132,810 miles and was repainted only once, in September 1947, while its wartime wooden seats were replaced just over two months later. *J. Cull*

1403-1406 (FOP 403-406)
Guy 'Arab' II; Gardner 5LW 7.0-litre engine; Weymann MoS H30/26R body; allocated by MoS 3.1943, es.11.1944, w 1.1949-12.1950

These four buses were built by Weymann to the same design as 1393-1400 and were equipped with wooden seats until their first overhaul in mid-1947. They were allocated initially to Perry Barr garage.

1403 (FOP 403)
The line of vehicles parked in Yardley Wood Road outside Yardley Wood bus garage isn't quite what it seems. 1403 (FOP 403), a brand new Weymann-bodied Guy 'Arab' II with the usual Gardner 5LW 7-litre diesel engine, heads a line-up of ten wartime buses on 1 November 1944. The picture was used for publicity in the local press, and it was inferred that these were the latest buses to be delivered. Certainly this was the first day in service for 1403, but a closer examination of the rest of the buses suggests that they were not new and had two different body manufacturers' products. Immediately behind the leading bus is 1376 (FOP 376),

another Guy 'Arab' II with a Weymann body, but already well over three months old. The next four are Park Royal-bodied Guys, while the last three in the row are more Weymann-bodied 'Arabs'. The chief distinguishing feature of the Weymann body was that the top of the offside cab windows went up almost to ceiling level, and was not lined up with the top of the windscreen nor the bottom of the canopy. In addition, when compared with a Park Royal body, the front profile was flat whereas the Park Royal body had a slightly curved and therefore more attractive profile. *Birmingham City Transport*

1407-1412 (FOP 407-412)
Guy 'Arab' II; Gardner 5LW 7.0-litre engine; Park Royal MoS H30/26R body; allocated by MoS 3.1943, es 6.1944-7.1944, w 1.1949-11.1950

These four buses were built by Park Royal to the same design as 1380-1383 and were equipped with wooden seats until their first overhaul in late-1946

1407 (FOP 407)

Above right Standing outside the entrance to Barford Street garage in 1949 is 1407 (FOP 407), the first of the batch, which had entered service in the early summer of 1944, months before the MoWT announced its 'relaxed' type of body. Looking smart after its repaint in March 1948, when it was equipped with upholstered seats from withdrawn pre-war stock, 1407 would stay in service until the end of May 1950, though it was 'parked up' for a further six weeks before being officially withdrawn in mid-July. Just visible inside the garage is 869 (BOP 869), one of Barford Street's allocation of Daimler COG5s. Barford Street opened as a garage in March 1925, and was converted from a factory. It remained open until 1955, when it was replaced by the new garage at Lea Hall, although much of the work done at Barford Street was on the Inner

Circle service and these schedules were transferred to Highgate Road and Liverpool Street. *B. W. Ware collection*

1408 (FOP 408)

Below left Coming out of Cattell Road at the Coventry Road junction in 1948, beneath the route 84 Stechford tram wiring, is 1408 (FOP 408), being employed on a driver training duty. It is passing the Greenway Arms at the apex of this important junction. In front of the pub was a large horse trough, which must have been one of the last to survive in Birmingham. The bus is negotiating not only the treacherous cobbled road surface but also the awkward junction. The busy A45 Coventry Road swings to the right of the public house and takes with it the Coventry Road trolleybus routes to Yardley, Sheldon and the Rover 'shadow' factory at Lode Lane, Solihull; the twin overhead wires can be seen above 1408. Following the bus in Cattell Road is an early post-war Austin K2 lorry, while behind the shops on the left is the 'Blues' St Andrew's football ground. *Author's collection*

1409 (FOP 409)

Below Standing at the Bundy Clock in Warwick Road outside the New Inns public house is 1409 (FOP 409), working on the 1A route to the City Centre by way of Moseley Village, and about to be overtaken by an earlier Weymann-bodied Guy 'Arab' II that is apparently working on the same service. The car in the foreground is an Austin 10hp four-door saloon, registered in Birmingham with a GOE mark in April 1946. Standing at the distant bus stop in Shirley Road outside the late—1920s mock-Tudor shops is one of Acocks Green garage's quirky-looking AEC 'Regent' 0961 RT types with four-bay-construction bodies, which were numbered 1631-1645 and, like the Austin 12, had GOE registrations. *Commercial postcard*

1413-1419 (FOP 413-419)
Daimler CWA6; AEC A173 7.58-litre engine; Park Royal MoS H30/26R body; allocated by MoS 5.1944 as Brush H30/26R, but body contract transferred to Park Royal; es 3.1945-5.1945, w 2.1949-3.1950

This batch of six buses was a continuation of the 1385-1392 class, with both chassis and body numbers that followed on exactly. The Park Royal bodies were again to the 'relaxed' design introduced by the MoS in December 1944, which included more opening saloon windows.

1414 (FOP 414)
Looking in need of some bodywork attention, 1414 (FOP 414) is parked in Washwood Heath yard on 22 April 1950. These Daimler CWA6s were identical to the 1385-1392 batch and had a similarly short life-span. A livery variation with some of the Park Royal-bodied Daimlers was the middle blue livery band going straight across below the front destination box. 1414 is displaying the destination blind for the 15 service to Church Road, Yardley, which was the short-working of the newly extended 15B route to Sheldon Heath Road, occurring on 23 January 1949. Parked behind is Metro-Cammell-bodied Daimler COG5 1154 (FOF 154), which had received the body from 1172 during 1948. *A. D. Packer*

1420-1425 (FOP 420-425)
Daimler CWD6; Daimler CD6 8.6-litre engine; Park Royal MoS H30/26R body; allocated by MoS 6.1944 as Brush H30/26R, but body contract was transferred to Park Royal; es 6.1945, w 1.1950-1.1951

The Park Royal bodies were to a 'relaxed' design that had been announced by the MoS in December 1944, although compared to the earlier bodies the rear dome was slightly less severe; numerically the body numbers continued from the previous batch of CWA6s. These were the first Daimler-engined wartime buses to be built and

1420 was the first Daimler CD6-engined chassis to be completed.

1423 (FOP 423)
On this vehicle, the black-painted radiator grill is a honeycomb pattern rather than the vertical-slatted version usually associated with the CWD6s – this is the way to identify the Daimler CWD6 from its wartime stable-mate. 1423 (FOP 423), which has been in service for just 20 days, stands in Old Square outside Crane's piano shop at the terminus of the 14 route on 20 June 1945. As usual with the Corporation wartime fleet, this bus only received one repaint, during April 1947, but during November 1946 a tantalising comment is recorded: 'Experimental engine fitted by Daimler'. It still didn't extend the life of 1423 as it was withdrawn in July 1950 after totalling 147,000 miles in service. *J. Cull*

1426-1431 (FOP 426-431)
Daimler CWA6; AEC A173 7.58-litre engine; Duple MoS H30/26R body; allocated by MoS 6.1944, es 1.1945-3.1945, w 2.1949-11.1950

These buses were equipped with wooden seats until their first overhaul in mid-1947.

1426 (FOP 426)
Top Holford Drive is a narrow lane off Aldridge Road and was almost within sight of Perry Barr garage. Between about 1948 and 1955 it was used to park up all the pre-war and wartime buses that were about to be sold to dealers; examples could stand at the Holford Drive disposal site for up to 18 months. The deeply upholstered seats on the upper deck of 1426 (FOP 426) had been fitted in December 1947 when it had received its only 'clean and varnish', which was Tyburn Road's phrase for a repaint; it was withdrawn from service on 30 April 1950. Buses were usually parked up for several weeks at their last operating garage, which in the case of 1426 was Liverpool Street, then on 20 July 1950 it was 'taken off strength for disposal' and a month later was sold to W. T. Bird for disposal. It has recently arrived at the Holford Drive site and still has recent timetable alteration notices in the windows. The characteristic features of the Duple body at this time were the thin body pillars, the raised bottom of the off-side driver's cab with the angled corner to the top of the driver's door, and the 'shell-backed' rear dome. *R. A. Mills*

1427, (FOP 427)
Middle When the Stechford tram services were converted to bus operation on 3 October 1948, the 90 tram service was replaced by the 53 bus route. This went through the back

streets of Digbeth by way of Fazeley Street, Great Barr Street and Garrison Lane, where 1427 (FOP 427) is travelling on its way into the city soon after the conversion to buses. It is passing a row of 1860s housing, while further back up the hill is the corner shop in Venetia Road. To the right are the Holmes, North, South, East and West, the city's first municipal flats, built in 1927 on land adjacent to St Andrew's football ground. They were three-storey buildings with Dutch-style gables and survive today as listed properties. The bus looks in fine fettle despite its withdrawal within the next two years, as it crosses over the recently abandoned tram tracks in Garrison Lane. *F. W. York*

1428 (FOP 428)
Bottom One of the neat yet uncompromising wartime Duple-bodied Daimler CWA6s, 1428 (FOP 428), is working on the 14B service to Kitts Green and Lea Village in about 1949. It is pulling away from the bus stop in Saltley Road at Nechells Place, and is about to cross Saltley Viaduct; on the right was the City Gas Works which gave off a constant, pungent smell of coal gas across the whole area. Like all the wartime Daimlers, 1428 had a Wilson pre-selector gearbox and a fluid flywheel and was a considerably better proposition to get away on a rising gradient such as this, when compared to one of the awkward manual gearboxes fitted to the contemporary Guy 'Arabs'. *S. E. Letts*

1432-1450 (FOP 432-450) Guy 'Arab' II; Gardner 5LW 7.0-litre engine; Park Royal MoS H30/26R body; allocated by MoS 6.1944, es 9.1944-12.1944; 1433 fitted with Brush MoS H30/21R body from SV 56 (OG 3639), new 9.1943 on 391 (OG 391), and converted to dual-control trainer 97, 6.1952-12.1964; 1434 became SV 94 1.1952 with similar Brush body from 452 (OV 4452), w 12.1964; w 1.1949-12.1950

This was the largest single batch of wartime buses allocated to Birmingham. They were equipped with wooden seats until their first overhaul.

1433 (FOP 433)

Above right The driver has walked to his cab after 'pegging the clock' at the Kings Head public house in Lordswood Road in about 1948. In the background the Speedy Valet Service shop is in Hagley Road, just two shops away from the junction with Bearwood Road. The bus, 1433 (FOP 433), is working on an Outer Circle shortworking to Harborne, where it was garaged. The neat lines of the Park Royal body rather hid the frequently poor quality of the unseasoned wood used in its composite construction. As Birmingham turned down a batch of metal-framed Northern Counties-bodied Daimler CWA6s, it was probable that the decision was made quite early on that the frail wartime composite bodies were not going to have a long life in the city. The recommendation appears to have been that the

Corporation should dispose of all the utilities because of the quality of their body build, irrespective of the body manufacturer, condition or age. All Birmingham's wartime buses received one overhaul and repaint, but after December 1948 this practice stopped and it was soon after that the first 'utilities' were taken out of service. 1433 went at the end of November 1950, but unusually had an after-life with the Corporation, being selected for conversion to a dual-control trainer. *Author's collection*

1434 (FOP 434)

Below In its last year before conversion to a dual-control trainer, 1434 (FOP 434) travels into the city passing the Westminster Bank and Miss Partridge's Babbette ladies hairdressing salon. Well-loaded and showing an anonymous 'CITY' service, it has just left Bearwood, in Hagley Road, on what looks like a 'three-bell load' – this was the conductor's signal to his driver that he was full up and that he need not stop for any waiting passengers, though the driver would have to stop if instructed to do so by the conductor. Although fitted with a Gardner 5LW 7.0-litre engine, the Guy 'Arab' chassis was not particularly underpowered and with a load like this could have a good turn of speed up to its governed engine speed. *S. E. Letts*

1437, 1440, etc

Above Despite the obvious difficulties of wartime, Birmingham's buses still managed to look smart. These six Guy 'Arab' IIs lined up in the entrance doors of Yardley Wood garage on 1 November 1944 are sparkling as four of them are virtually new and one has yet to earn a penny. With 'BIRMINGHAM CITY TRANSPORT' proudly emblazoned on the architrave, Yardley Wood was the newest of Birmingham's bus garages, opening during November 1938. 1403 (FOP 403), the fourth bus from the left, is a brand-new Weymann-bodied bus that will enter service later on this Wednesday morning. The first two buses on the left and the one on the extreme right (1437, 1440 and 1439 respectively) are literally days old, being from the 1432-1450 class with Park Royal bodies. The remaining two Weymann-bodied buses are 1375 and 1376 (FOP 375 and 376), just two and four months old. From the front, the body types could be distinguished by the angle of the cream below the windscreen, which married up with the bottom of the cream below the lower saloon windows. However, this was not always a good identifier as some of the Park Royal-bodied Guys had either deep cream waistbands (see 1395), or had minor individual variations, apparently at the whim of the coach painter on the day, after having their only overhaul and repaint at Tyburn Road Works. *Birmingham City Transport*

1450 (FOP 450)

Left The last bus in this class of 19, 1450 (FOP 450), which had entered service on 1 December 1944, is parked in front of the row of cottages in Harborne Lane opposite Selly Oak garage. Behind the bus are the cranes used by the Premier Woven Wire Mattress Company, which stood between the cottages and the Dudley No 2 canal. This utility Guy is working on a special learner duty on 20 March 1950, and is eight months away from withdrawal, during which time it managed another 9,000 miles to add to its already achieved 139,000 miles. The driving instructor gives the trainee driver some words of advice as he leans through the emergency window linking the cab with the lower saloon. *A. B. Cross*

1451-1453 (FOP 451-453) Daimler CWA6; AEC A173 7.58-litre engine; Duple MoS H30/26R body; allocated by MoS 6.1944, es 1.1945-3.1945, w 10.1949-7.1950

These three buses were a continuation of the 1426-1431 class, but had upholstered seats from new.

1452 (FOP 452)

The 1890s buildings in the Old Square had succeeded the town houses in what had been Birmingham's last central Georgian square, but these splendid Victorian premises would

only last another 14 or so years before being swept away in an ill-conceived 1960s scheme to make Old Square a traffic gyratory system as part of the Inner Ring Road scheme. The Duple body on 1452 (FOP 452) still looks smart from its 'clean and varnish' in November 1947. It is working on the 14B route, which at this time was being operated by Washwood Heath garage. After its sale in January 1950, the bus had a long life with four different operators, eventually

surviving until 1970 as an open-topper with Southend-on-Sea Corporation. Just alongside the bus is Crane's piano shop, with its canvas sunblinds pulled out over the pavement; they are selling both Philips and HMV television sets for the new BBC service, which had been opened on Saturday 17 December 1949 when the Sutton Coldfield television transmitter began beaming signals across the West Midlands. *R. Marshall*

1454-1455 (FOP 454-455) Guy 'Arab' II; Gardner 5LW 7.0-litre engine; Park Royal MoS H30/26R body; allocated by MoS 6.1944, es 12.1944, w 2.1949-12.1950

These two vehicles were equipped with wooden seats until their first overhaul in January 1947.

1455 (FOP 455)

The Corporation's last wartime Guy 'Arab' II, 1455 (FOP 455), was delivered in December 1944, some six months after being ordered for construction by the Ministry of Supply and allocated to the

Corporation by the Ministry of War Transport. Except for the 1359-1365 batch of Duple-bodied Daimler CWA6s of early 1944, all the Guys were in service by as much as six months prior to the arrival all the other deliveries from Daimler's Courtaulds factory in Whitmore Reans, Wolverhampton. Early in 1950, 1455 is travelling over the tram tracks in Rea Street having just passed the entrance to Midland Red's Digbeth garage. This garage opened on 3 January 1929 and by this time, with its open parking area fronting Digbeth, had a capacity for 140

buses; it had the highest annual mileage of any Midland Red garage because of its intensive work radiating from Birmingham. Although the Corporation Guy was typically being used as an instruction vehicle for trainee drivers, it was still in passenger service as it was still clocking-up around 1,500 miles per month. 1455 was taken out of service as early as New Year's Eve 1950, but having been stored in Holford Drive for three months, it went to Tyburn Road Works and had its good Gardner 5LW engine swapped for a poorer one prior to being sold. *A. B. Cross*

1456-1465 (FOP 456-465)
Daimler CWA6; AEC A173 7.58-litre engine; Park Royal MoS H30/26R body; allocated by MoS 1.1945, es 3.1945-5.1945, w 1.1949-11.1950

The Park Royal bodies were again to the 'relaxed' design introduced by the MoS in December 1944 and, for the first time with a wartime delivery, they had a full complement of half-drop opening saloon windows.

1459 (FOP 459)

Above Parked at the first bus stop in Victoria Square beyond Waterloo Street in the spring of 1946 is 1459 (FOP 459), less than a year old and working on the 15B service to Garretts Green Lane. This batch of buses reverted to the more attractive and brighter-looking livery with the deep cream waistrail, though the black-painted radiator rather dulled the whole effect. Once it has negotiated the awkwardly placed hand-cart, the bus will swing into New Street by way of Galloways Corner, which was part of the

block containing the offices of the Canadian Pacific Railway shipping line. The offices and bureau on the extreme right once belonged to the White Star Line, forever linked with the ill-fated RMS *Titanic*. Behind the bus, towards Bennett's Hill, is Colmore Row with a plethora of parked British-made cars from just before the Second World War, including, on the right, a Rover, and on the left an Austin Seven Ruby immediately behind the little Dennis 40/45cwt van, then a Singer Ten and a Morris Twelve. *Birmingham Central Reference Library*

1465 (FOP 465)

Below Standing at the northern terminus of the cross-city 15 and 16 service in Hamstead village is 1465 (FOP 465), delivered in November 1945. The CWA6 chassis was fitted with the six-cylinder 7.58-litre engine whose performance was usually considered to be smoother than the Gardner 5LW 7.0-litre unit found in the Guy 'Arabs'. Unfortunately, the Daimler had 'solid' engine mountings, producing a harsh level of vibration towards the top of the rev range, which rather detracted from the sophistication of

a vehicle equipped with a fluid flywheel and a pre-selector gearbox. The bus is in the old coal-mining village of Hamstead, on the northern flood plain of the River Tame, where mining started in 1880, quite late for the South Staffordshire Coalfield. It is waiting just beyond the last of the row of Victorian shops that included a hairdresser, a Post Office and a 'sweetie and fag' shop. Hamstead boasted an aerial ropeway whose buckets carried spoil and colliery waste from the mine to the nearby Hamstead Brickworks Quarry, which was located behind shops and the nearby Beaufort Arms public house. *Author's collection*

1466-1470 (FOP 466-470) Daimler CWA6D and rear axle; AEC A173 7.58-litre engine; Park Royal MoS H30/26R body; allocated by MoS 1.1945, es 11.1945-12.1945, w 7.1950-1.1951

The Park Royal bodies were again to the 'relaxed' design introduced by the MoS in December 1944 and, like their immediate predecessors, they had a full complement of half-drop opening saloon windows.

1468 (FOP 468)

At the rear of Tyburn Road Works a yard alongside the Birmingham & Fazeley Canal was used to park vehicles awaiting rectification or buses that had been examined and considered not worthy of remedial work. In early February 1951, 1468 (FOP 468) stands alongside 1470 (FOP 470), from the same batch, awaiting their fate. Next is 1720 (HOV 720), a Brush-bodied Leyland 'Titan' PD2/1 of 1948, and 1329 (FON 629), an 'unfrozen' Leyland-bodied Leyland 'Titan' TD7 that would be prematurely withdrawn

after being involved in a very bad accident in September 1951. The final identifiable bus is 1038 (CVP 138), the last of the 1937 batch of MCCW-bodied AEC 'Regent' 0661s; having only just been taken out of service, it still has its destination blinds. Both of the Daimlers had that company's rear axles, which were offered for the first time in early 1945 as an alternative to the usual Kirkstall-Forge units. Although they were both among the last 'utility' buses to remain in service and perhaps might have been thought as potential second-hand PSV bargains, neither ran again as passenger-carrying vehicles. They were sold to the Birmingham Co-Operative Society in May 1951, which cut them down to the upper saloon waistrail and used them as green-painted mobile shops. *R. Hannay*

1471-1474 (FOP 471-474) Daimler CWA6; AEC A173 7.58-litre engine; Brush MoS H30/26R body; allocated by MoS 1.1945, es 9.1945, w 2.1950-12.1950

The Brush bodies were again to the 'relaxed' design introduced by the MoS in December 1944 and, like their immediate predecessors, they had a full complement of half-drop opening saloon windows, but were the only wartime buses not to have opening ventilators in the upper saloon front windows.

1472 (FOP 472)

Above right After having several batches of wartime buses diverted from Brush Coachworks, the Corporation took four Daimler CWA6 chassis with these Loughborough-built bodies, although this was some nine months after being allocated. 1472 (FOP 472) is working on the 43 service to Nechells on Christmas Eve 1949. This was the penultimate development of Brush's interpretation of the wartime body, which was considerably more refined than the structures used to re-body 50 piano-front petrol-engined AEC 'Regents'. They had a slightly curved rear dome, several opening saloon windows on each side of each deck, and the deep cream waistrail. 1472 is unloading its passengers outside Lewis's department store in Old Square before doing a tight U-turn across Upper Priory to gain its stand outside Yates's seed shop. *Author's collection*

1473 (FOP 473)

Right As the Austin, probably a 14hp, travels away from the photographer, 1473 (FOP 473), with 'CITY' on the blind, is

working on a Lucas Works service in about 1949. The location is difficult to identify, but it is passing rows of well-to-do Victorian villas. Although only a few years old, the bus is already showing signs that all is not well with the framework behind the driver's door around the offside of the front bulkhead. Despite this, after its withdrawal the bus was exported to Ceylon, where it was rebodied as a single-decker and survived there until the summer of 1965. *E. Chitham*

1475-1479 (FOP 475-479)
Daimler CWA6D and rear axle; AEC A173 7.58-litre engine; Park Royal MoS H30/26R body; allocated by MoS 5.1945, es 2.1946, w 7.1950-1.1951

The Park Royal bodies were again to the 'relaxed' design introduced by the MoS in December 1944 and, like their immediate predecessors, they had a full complement of half-drop opening saloon windows.

1476 (FOP 476)
Top This bus looks much better for receiving a chrome radiator in June 1948 during its only repaint at Tyburn Road. 1476 (FOP 476) was another CWA6D with a Daimler rear axle assembly, which could be distinguished by having flatter and somewhat smaller-diameter half-shaft wheel hubs. It is waiting in Carrs Lane outside the Congregational Church when working on a Villa Park Football Special during the 1948 season. Also waiting for the rush of Villa Park-bound fans is a 1938 Daimler COG5 with a BRCW body and a 1948 Brush-bodied Leyland 'Titan' PD2.1. The Football Specials always parked on the wrong side of Carrs Lane opposite the regular service bus stops, so that they would not obstruct the trams and trolleybuses. Parked in front of FOP 476 is a 1939 Wolseley 16hp car. *S. N. J. White*

1477 (FOP 477)
Middle After withdrawal on the last day of January 1951, 1477 (FOP 477) was taken to Holford Drive prior to disposal; although appearing a little dusty, the Park Royal body looks worthy of further service. Parked alongside is 1464 (FOP 464), which was virtually the same except that it had a normal Kirkstall-Forge rear axle. Both buses were sold to Kearsey of Cheltenham after passing through the hands of W. T. Bird, the well-known Stratford-upon-Avon bus dealer. *P. Edgington*

1479 (FOP 479)
Bottom The 15A service was introduced in 1929 as the southbound journey between Hamstead and Barrows Lane, Yardley, and was linked to the 16 northbound service. On 20 March 1949 the 15A was extended to the late-1930s council estate at Whittington Oval just off The Meadway. 1479 (FOP 479) has just negotiated the traffic island in Hob Moor Road and is being enthusiastically overtaken by three young lads who are riding their drop-handlebar racing bikes; a Bradford CB shooting-brake is parked in Newbridge Road. The bus has just come down the steep hill from Little Bromwich and is about to cross the River Cole Valley. In the 1949-50 period the Hay Barnes recreation ground, off to the left, looked like a modern-day wind farm as in winter it contained a surfeit of netted soccer goalposts and imposingly tall H-shaped Rugby Union posts. The bus is travelling towards Wash Lane and, beyond that, the Yew Tree junction in South Yardley where the Outer Circle bus route was crossed. *D. Griffiths*

1480 (FOP 480)
Daimler CWA6; AEC A173 7.58-litre engine; Park Royal MoS H30/26R body; allocated by MoS 5.1945, es 2.1946, w 7.1950

The Park Royal body was again to the 'relaxed' design introduced by the MoS in December 1944 and, like its immediate predecessors, it had a full complement of half-drop opening saloon windows.

1480 (FOP 480)

What a difference three years makes! 1480 (FOP 480), the very last Birmingham bus delivered under wartime restrictions, entering service on 1 February 1946, waits outside the Star public house in Dale End. The angular lines of its body contrast with the stylish Metro-Cammell body of Daimler CVD6 1989 (HOV 989) behind it, which had entered service on 1 November 1949. The third bus is a petrol-engined AEC 'Regent', rebodied by Brush during the war and in its last throes before imminent withdrawal, being confined to short workings and Saturday excursions to Villa Park. 1480 would only last until the middle of July 1950, which all suggests that this football match took place on 21 January 1950, when, for the first time, tramcars did not provide the normal service extras for the Aston Villa faithful. *S. N. J. White*

GNE 247
Crossley DD42.1; Crossley HOE7 8.6-litre engine with Brockhouse-Salerni torque converter; Crossley H30/26R body; b 5.1944, demonstrated ?.1945

This was the prototype post-war Crossley double-decker design, and had the new Crossley HOE7 8.6-litre engine that had been developed by Crossley Motors during the latter part of the war.

GNE 247

With the chassis number 92901, GNE 247 came to Birmingham when it was still owned by Crossley Motors, although it was in this streamlined livery, which was the standard for Manchester Corporation. Its body was a standard pre-war MCCW-framed structure that had been finished by Crossley and looked very similar to the English Electric bodies bought in 1941 and 1942 and mounted on blitz-damaged Daimler COG5s and Leyland 'Titan' TD6cs. As the new-style post-war body design was not completed, GNE 247 got this 1939 one, which had been intended for Manchester's 1211. The Crossley was intended to be Manchester's 1217, but was renumbered 2960 as early as July 1947. *C. W. Heaps*

2.
1947–1954
REPLACING EVERYTHING WITH NEW BUSES

The first eight years after the end of the Second World War were extremely difficult ones for Birmingham City Transport. There were very few private cars, television would not begin in the West Midlands until 17 December 1949 and passenger numbers were rising rapidly, but the fleet of buses, trolleybuses and trams, although quickly repainted and brought back to a presentable condition, was generally in need of replacement.

The design of the post-war BCT body was a development of those built on the pre-war Daimler COG5s and some of the Leyland 'Titan' TD6cs. Initially the body contract was placed with Metro-Cammell, and these had the typical 'Birmingham' specification with idiosyncratic front profiles, straight staircases, elaborate body mouldings and high-quality interior fittings. Although Brush had built the post-war prototype body on 1235 (FOF 235), that company's interpretation of the BCT standard body was not acceptable and, after building bodies on the 100 Leyland 'Titan' PD2 Specials, 1656-1755, body contracts were placed elsewhere until a regular alternative supplier was found. Thus Park Royal, Leyland and Weymann bodies (in the case of Weymann, single-deckers) were produced with their standard outlines but with superimposed BCT features, which often resulted in these buses looking better than the 'BCT Standard' design. Birmingham even flirted briefly with Burlingham of Blackpool, but the City Transport Department eventually placed the order with Metro-Cammell. This need to have 'the Birmingham look' slowed down body production during the early post-war years when elsewhere most municipalities were willing to have what they could quickly acquire.

In 1946 the first motorbus contracts were placed for 175 new buses. These included 75 Daimler CVA6s and 75 Daimler CVG6s. Of the remainder, the 15 AEC 'Regent' III 0961RTs, which were delivered between July and October 1947, were the remnants of the provisional order placed in 1941, while a small batch of 10 prototypes of the new Crossley DD42/6s were all that was left of another provisional order for 40 Stockport-built buses. The first of the 175, 1481 (GOE 481), a CVA6, did not arrive until 20 June 1947, while the Crossleys, because of problems with bodybuilders and engines, did not start to enter service until May 1949.

As an interim measure to keep as many buses on the road as possible, the programme of swapping chassis and bodies, begun in 1941, was continued. In September 1941 the Transport Department purchased 20 new English Electric H28/26R bodies intended for Manchester Corporation's Daimler COG5s, which had been destroyed in an air-raid on Daimler's Radford Works in Coventry. Sixteen buses whose bodies had been destroyed on the night of 22-23 November 1940, when Hockley garage had been bombed, were rebodied, resulting in 12 Leyland 'Titan' TD6cs and four Daimler COG5s being fitted with these bodies. This allowed a float of four bodies to be created. In simple terms, body overhauls took longer than chassis overhauls, so in order to get buses back on the road quickly, when a chassis had completed its overhaul at Tyburn Road Works the next available overhauled body of comparable type and age was placed on it. Between 1941 and 1952 some 386 body swaps were completed, though after about 1948, when the body float of four had been used up, the general policy was to fit an overhauled Daimler COG5 chassis with a Metro-Cammell body and to scrap the less robust, though contemporary, Birmingham Railway & Carriage bodies, thus making one good bus out of two vehicles. In addition, 110 pre-war Metro-Cammell bodies renovated by Samlesbury Engineering between December 1947 and July 1949 were remounted on reconditioned Daimler COG5 chassis, which provided some cover as deliveries slowly began to improve. Yet by mid-1949, of the 1,100 new buses ordered, only 320 had been delivered.

There were 453 tramcars available for service on 1 January 1946 but it would be another fifteen months before the tram abandonment programme could be resumed. The three route groups for which closure dates had already been set prior to the Declaration of the Second World War were the first to be converted to buses. The Lodge Road 32 route was converted on 30 March 1947 and the Ladywood 33 service went on 31 August 1947 thus ending tramcar operation at Rosebery Street depot. Both services had been due to close with the Dudley Road services on 30 September 1939 but were reprieved. The Stechford tram services 84 and 90 were the routes which benefited because of the outbreak of war, having been pencilled-in for 1 April 1940 closure. These two routes had been the last extension on the BCT tram system, reaching their new reserved track terminus on 26 August 1928. These services from Coventry Road depot were closed on 2 October 1948. Vehicles from the 1948 HOV-registered Daimler CVD6 class were operated on the new Stechford bus services from Liverpool Street garage to Coventry Road schedules. This was the first post-war conversion where new buses had taken over from the trams.

At a meeting of the Transport Committee on 5 July 1949 the decision was made to rid Birmingham of the rest of its trams and, perhaps surprisingly, its profitable trolleybus service along Coventry Road to Sheldon via Small Heath and Yardley. By the date of this meeting there were

still only about 438 new buses in service. All post-war deliveries of buses up to Daimler CVG6 1917 were in service, with the exception of 1655, the solitary Brockhouse-Salerni Turbo-Transmitter-equipped Crossley DD42/6T, while all the 2131-2180 class of Leyland-bodied Leyland 'Titan' PD2/1s were running from Hockley garage.

The final abandonment dates for the tram route closures were 1 October 1949 for the Moseley Road group of services, 31 December 1949 for the 3X to Witton and the 6 route to Perry Barr, while on 30 September 1950 the inter-suburban 5 service between Lozells and Gravelly Hill and the two routes operated by Washwood Heath depot, the 8 to Alum Rock and the 10 to Washwood Heath, were converted to buses. The closure of the Coventry Road trolleybus routes took place on 30 June 1951, although the average age of the 'Silent Service' fleet was only 14 years. The reason was that, with only 74 trolleybuses in a fleet of 1700-plus motorbuses, it was not realistic to operate this 'system within a system'. The penultimate tram abandonments – the 36 route to Cotteridge and the two Bristol Road services, the 70 to Rednal and the 71 to Rubery – were to take place on 5 July 1952, the same date as London Transport's final tram abandonment. The final tram routes to be closed were the three Erdington group of services, to Erdington (2), Short Heath (78) and Pype Hayes (79). In order to achieve this removal of trams from the streets of Birmingham, 425 additional buses were required.

In addition, the decision was also made to dispose of all the pre-war buses, which by 1949 consisted of all the surviving Daimler COG5s, Leyland 'Titan' TD6cs and just five AEC 'Regent' 0661s and five Leyland 'Titan' TD4cs. In 1946, 22 pre-war buses were taken out of service, in 1947 it was 88 buses, 133 went in 1948, 196 in 1949, and a colossal 220 pre-war buses in 1950. Many of these pre-war vehicles were to have long lives in the second-hand market. By 1950 all the early 1934-35 Daimlers had been taken out of service, while the withdrawal of the pre-war Daimler COG5 single-deckers, which would be completed during the following year, was begun. Bus withdrawals for 1951 only numbered 15, in 1952 there were 97 pre-war buses taken out of stock, in 1953 there were 25 withdrawals, 172 went in 1954, and in 1955 27 pre-war buses were withdrawn. This left just 42 Daimler COG5s in store to be overhauled and resurrected, beginning in June 1957 when 1082 (CVP 182) was returned to service. The two utility-bodied 'unfrozen' Leyland 'Titan' TD7s also were withdrawn, though the six Leyland-bodied TD7s of 1942 and the four 8-foot-wide Daimler COG6s were destined to remain in service until the last of the MOF-registered buses entered service in October 1954.

Even more surprising was the decision to withdraw all the 149 wartime Guy 'Arab' Is and IIs as well as the Daimler CWG5, CWA6 and CWD6 buses. It had been briefly considered in 1947 whether the wartime Daimlers, with their Wilson pre-selector gearboxes and fluid flywheels, were worth rebodying, but the decision was made to 'buy new'. This choice would come to haunt a later generation of the Transport Committee, as by the early 1960s, with dramatically dropping passenger numbers, the Corporation found itself with too many mid-life buses in good condition, mostly of the same age, in a market where the resale value of a bus was very poor, since London Transport had found similar problems and was flooding the second-hand market with redundant eight-year-old AEC 'Regent' RTs.

The withdrawal of Birmingham's 149 buses built to MoWT standards between March 1942 and February 1946 began in 1948 with two Guy 'Arab' Is. As deliveries of new buses increased, so the withdrawal of these 'utilities' grew apace. In 1949 26 Daimlers and the remaining four Guy 'Arab' Is and 31 Guy 'Arab' IIs were withdrawn, while in 1950 the last of the trio of Daimler CWG5s, 27 CWA6s and five CWD6s joined all the remaining 47 Guy 'Arab' IIs to be withdrawn. This left just four Daimler CWA6s and two CWD6s to survive to be withdrawn in January 1951. The rate at which buses were taken out of service is well shown by the life of 1475, a Daimler CWA6D with a Park Royal body, which entered service on 1 February 1946 and was withdrawn just 41 months later on 14 July 1949, having recorded only 116,246 miles!

There was never a policy to withdraw one vehicle and replace it with another, though the gamble to abandon the trams, the trolleybuses, the pre-war bus fleet and the wartime buses was dependant upon the delivery of new buses at a rate that would support this amount of vehicle replacement. This somewhat profligate policy involved the purchase of a total of 1,718 double-deck buses as well as 35 single-deckers in a space of eight years.

For the record, between 1947 and 1954 Birmingham City Transport acquired no fewer than 75 Daimler CVA6s, 412 CVG6s, 438 CVD6s and one Daimler lightweight CLG5, making a post-war Daimler total of 926. Daimler had been Birmingham's preferred chassis manufacturer since 1934, although in 1938 the specially designed Leyland 'Titan' TD6c became the preferred alternative choice. After the Second World War BCT initially went back to Leyland Motors, and was in fact the recipient of the second and last prototype Leyland PD2, which was numbered 296 (HOJ 396). One hundred PD2 Specials with Brush bodies appeared, and two batches of 50 PD2/1s with either fairly normal Park Royal or Leyland bodies.

When the quality of the long-delayed Crossley bodies was seen, Birmingham realised that it had its urgently required secondary body supplier, which also had the capacity to build large quantities of bodies. As a result of their somewhat clandestine demonstration of GNE 247 in 1945, Crossley Motors eventually bodied the 260 production-batch Crossley DD42/6s and all the bodies for the two batches of 125 Daimler CVG6s of 1952-54. The Crossley Motors order for 260 DD42/6 chassis with Crossley H30/24R bodies became the largest post-war order ever placed with the company for the home market. Unfortunately, as Crossley was now controlled by ACV, which had announced its intention to end indigenous Crossley production, BCT had to look elsewhere again. The wartime Guy 'Arab' chassis had proved itself to be particularly robust, so Guy Motors was approached to build a heavily modified, pre-selector gearbox version of its 'Arab' III double-decker chassis to Birmingham's own specification. In addition, it had to have a concealed radiator, which had originally been conceived in BCT's drawing office.

As if to compete with the concealed-radiator buses being introduced by the neighbouring Midland Red Company, Guy Motors was able to do all the mock-up work for the new front end, only for Crossley to put into service in February 1950 bus 2426 (JOJ 426), the first of the last 100 Crossley-bodied DD42/6s that had been intended to have the 'New Look' front. Crossley stole a march on Guy by more than three months with its version of the 'New Look' front, so called because it resembled a Christian Dior narrow-hipped and ankle-length skirt … apparently! Eventually Guy built a total of 301 'Arab' III Specials or IVs between 1950 and 1954, all but one having Metro-Cammell bodies. The odd one belonged to one of the three lightweights bought between 1952 and 1954, which experimented with the concept of bringing the weight of an unladen Birmingham bus down from around 8 tons to something about 15cwt less in order to reduce the beginning-to-spiral running costs. 3001 (LOG 301) was the Guy 'Arab' IV with a Saunders-Roe body, while 3002 (LOG 302) was one of only two Daimler CLG5 chassis ever built, and this had a very lightweight Metro-Cammell pre-production 'Orion' body. The final bus of this trio was 3103 (MOF 103), which was a lightened version of the standard Crossley-bodied Daimler CVG6. All these buses worked from Acocks Green garage for almost their entire lives, but no new orders were ever placed.

By October 1954 the Birmingham bus fleet was totally renewed with smart-looking buses that had improved services and had eliminated nearly all the pre-war and all the wartime stock. The trams and trolleybuses had disappeared in this striving for modernity, which, as a by-product, had made Birmingham the largest city in the world not to have any form of electric-powered road public transport.

1481-1555 (GOE 481-555) Daimler CVA6; AEC A173 7.58-litre engine; MCCW H30/24R body, es 6.1947-11.1947, w 2.1961-7.1967

These were the first post-war buses to enter service. The CVA6 chassis was a comparative rarity, with only about 325 being built. It was a development of the wartime CWA6 model, but had flexible engine mountings. This batch of 75 was the second largest to be built, exceeded only by the 96 examples for Coventry City Transport. The 7ton 12cwt Metro-Cammell bodies (three-quarters of a ton more than the standard pre-war Daimler COG5) were unique to BCT; they had basically pre-war fixtures and fittings in both saloons, but although the general shape was to become the post-war standard, the bodies had very thin

window pillars and recessed window-pans that were not repeated on subsequent MCCW bodies for BCT. This class introduced the raked windscreen, designed to prevent the reflection of the lower saloon lights onto the windscreen at night

1482 (GOE 482)

The second member of the first post-war class of 75 CVA6s was 1482 (GOE 482). Their extra weight was in part due to the more robust post-war chassis, but the body was also heavier and had what would remain the Birmingham standard styling until the first buses with the 'New Look' concealed radiator were delivered, with the raked rather than angled windscreen being perhaps the most characteristic feature. 1482 is in Great Hampton Street on a 'CITY' route working into the city centre; this destination display was only used as the shortworking of the 29 route from the Circle, Kingstanding. The bus is letting off passengers at the bus stop just before Great Hampton Row. Although behind the bus is Snape's chemist shop, most of the premises in this area, at the edge of the famous Jewellery Quarter, were devoted to the jewellery trade and silversmithing. *F. W. York/R. F. Mack*

1495 (GOE 495)

Top 1495 entered service on 18 July 1947 working from Harborne garage, where it remained until it moved to Birchfield Road garage in 1954. In January 1961 it returned to Harborne until withdrawal on 31 December 1961, having totalled almost 387,000 miles in service. It is

during its second sojourn at Harborne garage that it is seen travelling through Victoria Square when working on the 12 service to Bartley Green. It is following a May 1938-registered Ford 7W Ten saloon, which was the precursor to the Ford Prefect E93A. Towering over the bus is the smoke-blackened Darley Dale limestone pillars of the Birmingham Council House, designed in 1874 by Yeoville Thomason and completed in 1879 as part of Joseph Chamberlain's scheme to give the then growing industrial town of Birmingham a sense of Civic Pride. *F. W. York/R. F. Mack, courtesy of BaMMOT*

1513 (GOE 513)

Middle The first statue in the United Kingdom to commemorate the victory of the Battle of Trafalgar and the death of Admiral Lord Horatio Nelson on 21 October 1805 was erected in Birmingham in 1809. 1513 (GOE 513) is picking up passengers opposite the statue outside the temporary shops in the war-damaged Bull Ring. On the left are the Doric columns of the roofless Market Hall, designed in a classic style by Charles Edge and officially opened on 12 February 1835. It was partially destroyed during the night of 25-26 August 1940, leaving it as a shell. The Board Inn on

the corner of Phillips Street and all the war-weary buildings on the left would be swept away when the Bull Ring was reconstructed in the early 1960s. 1513 is working on the cross-city 29A service, the second longest bus route in Birmingham, the famous 26-mile Outer Circle 11 route being the longer by about 6 miles. The use of Birchfield Road garage's Daimler CVA6 on the 29A was perhaps surprising as these buses only had the small 7.58-litre AEC engine, which made their progress rather more steady than sparkling. At the top of High Street, behind the post-war bus, is 1024 (CVP 124), a 1937 Metro-Cammell-bodied Daimler COG5 being used on a driver training duty. *Birmingham Central Reference Library, Local Studies*

1549 (GOE 549)

Bottom Coming towards the City on 2 May 1963 on the long cross-city 29 service is 1549 (GOE 549). It is in Stratford Road, Sparkhill, near Showell Green Lane and opposite the showrooms of Lincoln Street Motors, with a December 1961-registered Austin A40 Farina and a brand-new Austin Seven on the forecourt. The long climb from Springfield passing Sparkhill Park was a struggle for a fully loaded Daimler CVA6, so it must have been quite a relief for the driver that he was only about a third full. However, he has managed to attract an Austin A40 Somerset and a much newer Austin Cambridge A60, while taking up the rear is an eight-wheel Guy 'Invincible' with a comparatively rare Willenhall-built cab. *W. Ryan*

1556-1630 (GOE 556-630)
Daimler CVG6; Gardner 6LW 8.4-litre engine; MCCW H30/24R body; es 10.1947-6.1948, w 12.1961-10.1966

These were the post-war equivalent of the pre-war Daimler COG5 and, together with the later HOV-registered batch, became the real workhorses of the early post-war bus fleet. They weighed 7¼ tons, giving them a similar power-to-weight ratio to the COG5s. These 75 vehicles had a finalised design of Metro-Cammell bodywork with thicker window pillars, which was to be continued on all subsequent deliveries of exposed-radiator BCT Daimlers. Because of the need to obtain quicker deliveries of buses, Edinburgh Corporation bought 62 CVG6s and 10 CVD6s with this style of Birmingham-style body, while Newcastle purchased a further 14. During body construction there appears to have been an error, with four of the latter receiving bodies intended for Birmingham. As a result, the last four, 1627-1630, were built to the slightly modified specification of the 1844-1930 batch and were delivered four months after the rest.

1558 (GOE 558)
Above On 6 April 1960, a very rainy Wednesday, 1558 (GOE 558) travels into Bristol Street on its way into the city on the 45 service from West Heath by way of Kings Norton, Cotteridge and the A441 Pershore Road. The conversion of the Cotteridge 36 tram route to motorbus operation had taken place on 6 July 1952, using a batch of around 20 of these early numbered exposed-radiator GOE-registered buses, which were then about four years old. 1558 was one of them, and it stayed at Cotteridge for more than nine years until replaced by Guy 'Arab' III Specials from the 2526 class. The traffic lights in the distance are at the junction with Belgrave Road; this junction, together

with the early-Victorian retail premises on the left, were all swept away when the Middle Ring Road was built in the late 1960s. *Author's collection*

1575 (GOE 575)
Below The 1920s municipal housing estates in Kingstanding and Weoley Castle were the first in the city not to be served by trams. Buses first arrived in Weoley Castle on 17 October 1932, but as the population and size of the estate grew, so did the plethora of bus routes. The post-war expansion of bus services into the large Weoley Castle Estate became very complicated, with several variations of the 20, 21 and the later 22 services criss-crossing it. It is 20 July 1957, the last day of the original 20 service, which is duly recorded in the posters in the window next to the platform of 1575 (GOE 575), loading in Weoley Castle Square. The 20 route had its City terminus in Suffolk Street and went via Harborne to these large green-painted shelters in front of the shops around the Square, then meandered its way to the terminus in Chapel Lane, Selly Oak. The vehicle shows off the characteristically long bonnet accommodating the long Gardner 6LW engine when fitted to a Daimler chassis. Not many buses in this class had modifications, but 1575 was the first in the BCT fleet to be fitted with flashing rear indicator arrows alongside the number plate. *B. W. Ware*

1605 (GOE 605)

Above Working on the 37 service along Stratford Road, 1605 (GOE 605) stands alongside the Bundy Clock at the bottom of the hill in Carrs Lane where the driver will 'peg' his departure on the long run to the city boundary at Hall Green. This Highgate Road garage-based bus is waiting to leave during the last week of operation of the Coventry Road trolleybus services in June 1951. The 37's destination display was perhaps the least informative of them all, showing just 'HALL GREEN'. To the rear of the bus is the mock-Tudor frontage of the Corner public house, while alongside the bus are advertising hoardings hiding the still derelict plots caused by wartime bombing. *E. Chitham*

1618 (GOE 618)

Below This bus looks in remarkably good condition as it stands driverless in Corporation Street during the mid-afternoon of Sunday 4 September 1966. Except for the replacement of the trafficators with flashing indicators and the small black waistrail fleet numbers, introduced in 1960, these MCCW-bodied buses were hardly altered during their long lives, which is a testament to getting the design right in the first place. 1618 (GOE 618) is waiting for its slot in the timetabled departures from Old Square. It was frequently better to park the bus outside the Gazette Buildings, the offices and print works for the *Birmingham Gazette*, *Despatch* and *Sunday Mercury* newspapers because it was less congested than Old Square. The bus is being employed on the 14E service to Lea Hall and Kitts Green and was one of the last 21 of the class all withdrawn on 31 October 1966, a few weeks after this photograph was taken. *J. H. Taylforth collection*

1631-1645 (GOE 631-645) AEC 'Regent' 0961RT; AEC A204 9.6-litre engine; Park Royal H29/25R body; es 7.1947-10.1947, w 9.1962-2.1964

These were the most idiosyncratic-looking buses built for BCT, as well as being the largest batch of the 60 'Provincial' 3RT-type chassis to be constructed. Their delivery arose from the demonstration of RT 19 (FXT 194) in 1941, as well as the intended order for 15 AEC 'Regent' 0661s due to be delivered in 1942, which was never even placed because of wartime production curtailment. The bodies were the only ones ever built for Birmingham to have four-bay construction and were a version of Park Royal's 'thin-pillar' design. They were a strange amalgamation of the standard Park Royal body and BCT requirements, having tall raked windscreens, angled L-shaped staircases and headlights at different heights. They were also the first buses in the fleet to have air-brakes. The RTs were allocated to Acocks Green garage throughout, although 1643-1645 spent about two years at Barford Street from 1948. Because of their non-standard layout they were rarely allowed to operate on the Outer Circle 11 service, where drivers from other garages would not have been passed out to drive them. By the time of their withdrawal, virtually no two buses of the batch were the same as they were used extensively as test-beds for brakes, exhaust and cooling systems, and gearboxes.

1631 (GOE 631)

Top These 15 buses, with their powerful 9.6-litre engines, air-operated pre-selector gearboxes and air-brakes, were something of a mechanical nightmare for Acocks Green's garage mechanics, while their appearance was a curious mix of BCT features grafted rather uncomfortably on to the early Park Royal metal-framed bodywork. The first of the batch, 1631 (GOE 631), has just passed beneath the skeleton of what would become the impressive arc of buildings along the south side of Smallbrook Ringway. Preparation for the construction of the Inner Ring Road around the city centre began on 8 March 1957 when the Minister of Transport, the Rt Hon Harold Watkinson MP, blew up a wall near the junction of the Horse Fair and Smallbrook Street and managed to put a press photographer, hit by flying debris, in hospital. Smallbrook Ringway was the first section to open, and on 8 April 1959 Britain's first pedestrian subway as the only way to cross a road was opened between Hill Street and Hurst Street. The curious twin pairs of raked columns supporting the Ringway Centre building over Hurst Street still look impressive today, while a long-forgotten fact is that during its three years of construction, its builders, Laing, never once closed the roadway. About a year before the subway was opened, 1631 is working on the 32 service to the Gospel Lane estate on the borders of Acocks Green and Hall Green. It has recently lost its rear wheel discs, and positively sparkles in the sunshine. *A. B. Cross*

1636 (GOE 636)

Above Coming down the Camp Hill Flyover when working on the 44A route to Lincoln Road North, Acocks Green, is 1636 (GOE 636). The temporary flyover was opened on 15 October 1961 and was not demolished until 1986, which isn't bad for a short-term structure with a projected life of just seven years. It carried outward-bound traffic from High Street, Bordesley, over the junction with Coventry Road and into Camp Hill, reaching ground level outside Dowding & Mills' electrical rewinds company. And it worked! Traffic congestion was considerably reduced, and it was only when the structure was deemed to be time- rather than life-expired that it was demolished. It was quite worrying to drive a half-cab double-decker over the flyover as it was only about 9 feet wide, and to judge the turn to the right at the top when driving at about 25mph was extremely difficult. For some strange reason, 1636 had the upper part of the first window on the offside of the lower saloon panelled over. *L. Mason*

1637 (GOE 637)

Below The AEC 'Regent' III 0961 RTs were striking-looking vehicles, although the small-diameter front tyres and the headlights being at different levels did little to enhance their appearance. At the rear of the offside was the tall and somewhat narrow staircase window, behind which was a standard Park Royal L-shaped staircase that was both steep and came well on to the platform, making it unpopular with crews and passengers alike, who were used to the standard Birmingham straight staircase. The rumour was that the RTs were allocated to Acocks Green garage so that they could work on the prestigious 1A route through Moseley and Edgbaston and the General Manager, Mr A. C. Baker, could monitor them in service. This must have been a real bind for the garage staff as Mr Baker lived in Wake Green Road, which today is still a prestigious suburban road passing through the leafier parts of Moseley. 1637 (GOE 637) is travelling along Summer Road, Acocks Green, in July 1954 when working on the 1A service. It is approaching its home garage where it will turn right into Westley Road and speed down the hill to its terminus in Acocks Green Village. It is still sporting its rear wheel discs, which were always a feature of the RT family in London. At about this time there was a particularly unpleasant accident with an aluminium wheel trim coming loose, and the decision was made to remove them from all the 'New Look'-front buses that had them on both the front and rear wheels in order to enhance their appearance. It seems that the RTs were somehow overlooked, and when the rest of the fleet lost their silver and black wheel trims, the AECs hung on to theirs until about 1958. *R. Knibbs*

1642 (GOE 642)

Bottom The RTs were extensively used as experimental test-beds, particularly for modifications to their air-brake system, which seemed to prove particularly troublesome in a fleet where the triple-servo vacuum reigned supreme. 1642 (GOE 642) was fitted with disc brakes and was then taken to the MIRA test-track near Nuneaton for braking trials. On its way back, a driver who was unfamiliar with that part of deepest Warwickshire managed to drive the unfortunate 1642 under a low bridge, causing extensive damage to the front of the upper saloon. The bus spent eight months in Tyburn Road Works during 1960 and, somewhat surprisingly in view of its impending withdrawal, was returned to service sporting the most hideous rebuild imaginable! It is seen in Hurst Street having left the bus stop outside the Birmingham Hippodrome Theatre, which is where the distant Daimler CVD6 working on the 49B route is standing. By now fitted with the quite awful-looking front windows, 1642 is overtaking a well-appointed Armstrong-Siddeley Sapphire 346 saloon of 1953 parked outside the rather 'seedy' Empire Commercial Hotel on the corner of Thorp Street. Despite its accident and long time under repair, 1642 amassed some 355,000 miles in service. *R. F. Mack*

1646-1654 (GOE 646-654)
Crossley DD42/6; Crossley HOE7/4B 8.6-litre crossflow engine (1646/48/50-54), Crossley HOE7/5B 8.6-litre downdraught engine (1647/49); Crossley H30/24R body; es 5.1949-7.1949, w 6.1964-12.1964

Although ordered in 1946 as a result of the demonstration of GNE 247 two years earlier, Crossley Motors had been promised by BCT an order for 40 chassis in 1942, which obviously could not be fulfilled. The chassis were delivered to Liverpool Street garage while negotiations with Brush, who were to body them, broke down and a new contract was placed with Crossley Motors. Problems were also incurred with the new post-war Crossley engine, which further delayed their delivery. Two of the 1646-1654 batch were retrospectively fitted with the newly ACV-modified downdraught engine in August 1949. They were the first post-war buses to have a manual gearbox, although this was a synchromesh unit that had been developed especially for BCT.

1647 (GOE 647)

Top An almost new 1647 (GOE 647) is lying over in Church Road, South Yardley, opposite the Yew Tree public house, having worked on the 15A route; the row of 1920s mock-Tudor shops includes Harper's, a drapery shop, while the parking area in front was, in 1949, being used by Corporation buses. The first bus in the queue is 1362 (FOP 362), a 1945 Daimler CWA6 with a Duple body that is in its last year in service. Parked behind the Crossley in Church Road is a 1938 Morris Eight Series II saloon. 1647 entered service on 11 June 1949 and was finished to exhibition standards; its body was the first in the BCT fleet to have sliding ventilators as well as several other features that were peculiar to this bus, including being the only exposed-radiator bus to be fitted with decorative wheel trim discs on the front and rear wheels. It still has its original

thin-top radiator, which was unique to this batch of ten, while it also carries a radiator route slip board that supposedly added information to that on the destination blind. This bus was fitted with one of the more powerful pre-production prototype HOE7/5B downdraught engines and as such was effectively the prototype for the 2396-2425 class of exposed-radiator Crossleys. *D. Griffiths*

1648 (GOE 648)

Above This was the third of the prototype ten Crossley DD42/6s with Crossley 54-seat bodywork. They weighed in at slightly over 8tons 4cwt, making them 1½ tons heavier than the earlier Daimler CVA6s. All that extra weight caused them to 'puff a bit' when fully laden as they only had the 8.6-litre Crossley HOE7/4B crossflow engine which 'promised a lot but gave very little' (G. Hilditch). However, they did have the advantage of a four-speed synchromesh gearbox, which although obviously not a Wilson pre-selector unit, was a very easy manual gearbox to operate in service. 1648 is leaving the 56 route terminus in Coleshill Road, and has acquired a radiator from one of the large production batch of exposed-radiator Crossleys. Contrary to the destination blind, this terminus was neither in Castle Bromwich, which was over a mile away, nor Newport Road, the road from which the Standard Eight, Ford Consul, Morris Minor 1000 and Austin A55 Cambridge are emerging! *1685 Group*

1651 (GOE 651)

The 1646-1655 class of GOE-registered Crossleys could always be recognised from the production batch of 160 exposed-radiator buses by having a straight bottom to the nearside front mudguard. 1651 (GOE 651), sporting a later radiator, is working on the City Circle route in the autumn of 1963. It is approaching the Summer Lane junction in

New John Street West, having just left the stop in front of the impressive Victorian premises of Brandauer & Co, steel pen manufacturers. The City Circle 19 route was introduced on 2 March 1932 to serve the inner areas of the city. At this time, whole swathes of these central districts were tightly packed with back-to-back courtyard slums, mid-19th-century terraced housing or factories. After the

redevelopment of the Central Development Areas and the changes to the former industrial landscape as factories closed or moved to the newer premises being built in suburban industrial estates, the City Circle became less useful. Despite the needs of Birmingham's inner city industry, it was reduced to peak hours only as early as 25 September 1939. Although it did good business until the late 1950s, after that it just withered away as its main sources of revenue disappeared, leaving areas in both Aston and Hockley as open derelict land awaiting redevelopment. A remnant of the 19 was still operated by West Midlands PTE until October 1981. *1685 Group*

1655 (GOE 655)
Crossley DD42/6T; Crossley HOE7/5B 8.6-litre downdraught engine; Crossley H30/24R body; es 9.1949, w 12.1964

1646 was numerically the first of the new Crossley chassis, with chassis number 94801. After being stored in Liverpool Street it was returned to Crossley Motors where it was fitted with probably the third HOE7/5B downdraught engine to be placed in a double-deck chassis. It also had a Brockhouse-Salerni 'Turbo Transmitter' torque-converter, offered by Crossley Motors as an automatic-style alternative to a normal clutch and gearbox. 1655 was the only Birmingham Crossley to have this form of transmission, and continued the city's interest in

torque-converter gearing, used extensively in the pre-war Leyland 'Titan' TD6cs. 1646 was less than successful and the torque-converter was removed during September 1951.

1655 (GOE 655)

One can almost smell the new paint as 1655 (GOE 655) waits at the South Yardley terminus of the 15B route in Garretts Green Lane at the junction with Sheldon Heath Road in September 1949. The wide open spaces in the distance show that this was before the huge Garretts Green Technical College was built. After a number of changes in name and function, it is now East Birmingham College. 1655 entered service on 7 September 1949, some two months after the last of the other prototype Crossleys; it

could always be identified because the oil reservoir for the 'Turbo-Transmitter' was mounted on the front bulkhead. The bus was not a success, and could always be distinguished by a constantly revving engine, a lot of whirring and a distinct lack of forward motion commensurate to the amount of mechanical activity. In other words, the 'turbo did not transmit'! Crossley Motors removed the torque-converter on 18 September 1951, by which time 1655 had surprisingly covered 48,901 miles. *Author's collection*

296 (HOJ 396)
Leyland 'Titan' PD2;
Leyland 0.600 9.8-litre
engine; Leyland H30/26R
body; es 9.1947, w 10.1967

This was the second prototype Leyland PD2, the first being chassis EX1, registered CVA 430. EX2, completed at the end of June 1947, was given the chassis number 470848. It had a Leyland PD1-style body altered around the front of the cab, and was the first to have the lower cab apron below the windscreen finishing halfway down the offside mudguard, whereas CVA 430 and the PD1 had the apron overlapping the offside mudguard. Registered HOJ 396, the bus was given the next fleet number after the 1939 batch of Leyland 'Titan' TD6cs.

large brass-rimmed PD1-type headlights. It was also the only Birmingham bus to have 56 seats. *D. Griffiths*

296 (HOJ 396)

Above right BCT had been a valued customer of Leyland Motors in 1938, ordering the specially designed 'Titan' TD6c to its own specification. Having purchased all 135, the thinking was that in the post-war world Birmingham would again use Leyland as its alternative supplier. Thus the new large 9.8-litre PD2 was seen as an ideal model for Birmingham. Only two PD2 chassis were built, and the second, originally numbered EX2 and the only PD2 to be given a normal Leyland chassis number, was completed at the end of July 1947. The bus was delivered to BCT in the third week of September and entered service on Monday 29th; registered HOJ 396 and numbered 296, it became the only post-war bus not to be numbered in the main fleet sequence. It is standing in Nelson Road, Witton, waiting for the crowds to leave the 'Temple of Dreams' (the location shown on the destination blind!). This prototype Leyland could be easily identified when new as it carried a pair of rather splendid

296 (HOJ 396)

Below This bus was allocated to Yardley Wood garage for all its life, where it was a regular performer on the 24 service to Warstock. In about 1959 it crosses the traffic lights at Wake Green Road, Moseley, travelling into the city along the arboreal Yardley Wood Road. Initially 296 shared Yardley Wood garage with the first 50 of the Brush-bodied Leyland PD2 Specials. By 1959 it had been repainted into the standard fleet livery with two full-depth blue bands, and at first glance looked like a member of Hockley garage's 2131 class, though its registration number plate was carried below the windscreen and the arrangement of its half-drop opening saloon windows was different. It had to be manned by tall conductors as the platform bell was very difficult to reach. It was the first post-war vehicle to operate for 20 years, although it only achieved 312,000 miles in service. *F. W. York/R. F. Mack, courtesy of BaMMOT*

1656-1755 (HOV 656-755)
Leyland 'Titan' PD2 Special; Leyland 0.600 9.8-litre engine; Brush H30/24R body; es 3.1948-5.1949, w 8.1961-10.1968

These were among the first Leyland 'Titan' PD2s to be built, and although they were PD2.1s, the chassis had modifications to BCT specifications, thus the PD2 Special designation. These were the first production metal-framed Brush bodies, and were very similar to the post-war prototype fitted in 1946 to Daimler COG5 1235. All the 40 other Brush bodies to this design were mounted on AEC 'Regent' 0961 chassis and did not feature the BCT straight staircase. They were also the last bodies built for BCT by Brush as, although their quality was excellent, a number of mistakes were made, not the least being that the first 80 bodies had their patterned moquette put on sideways! The bodywork was the first to be delivered with a twin-skinned upper deck ceiling, which included both front and rear domes, but they were given pre-war-style twin emergency windows. 1735 was the only one of the batch to be fitted with the GB74 constant mesh gearbox.

1656 (HOV 656)

Below Waiting at the original terminus of the 13A route at the bottom of the hill in School Road at the Priory Road

terminus in Yardley Wood is 1656 (HOV 656), the first of the 100 PD2 Specials with the handsome Brush H30/24R body. The Swanshurst, Billesley and Trittiford areas of Yardley Wood had been developed as suburbs in the 1920s and were noted for their extensive areas of wide green open space. The urgent need to provide housing for families displaced from the inner areas by German air bombardment made it an ideal suburb in which to build the factory-made 'prefabs'; 4,625 were built in Birmingham, and a few are seen opposite the bus terminus turning circle. 1656 was delivered from the Brush Coachworks factory at Loughborough in February 1948 and entered service on 1 March, some five months before the next bus. It had various detailed differences to the rest of the class including the upper saloon handrail being mounted across rather than below the front windows and the banding around the front bulkhead above the bonnet. The positioning of the number plate just below the radiator header tank was also originally found on the next three buses when they were new. *Author's collection*

1657 (HOV 657)

Bottom left The PD2s were synonymous with the long 29A route as their 'long-legged' performance was well suited to this cross-city service, operated by both Yardley Wood's and Perry Barr's allocations of the class. 1657 (HOV 657) is working to the Hall Green terminus in Baldwins Lane and is in Stratford Road, Sparkhill, at the bus stops between St John's Road and Baker Street in about 1958. A sign of the times is that Harmer's Fashions has closed and is being converted into an electrical appliance shop selling televisions, refrigerators and washing-machines. Behind the bus is the Salvation Army Hall of 1908 on the site of the former coaling depot for the steam trams of CBT, whose 'shufflers' were replaced on 31 December 1906. Above the row of late-Victorian shops is the buttressed tower and spire of St John's Church, Sparkhill, dating from 1905, though the rest of the brick and terracotta Parish Church was built in 1888-89 to the designs of W. Martin and J. H. Chamberlain, a prominent partnership of Birmingham-based architects. The church stands at the top of the steep escarpment of Spark Hill at 425 feet above sea level, which would have held no problems for the powerful 9.8-litre-engined bus. *A. B. Cross*

1719 (HOV 719)

Opposite top Alma Street got its name from the Battle of Alma, which took place during the Crimean War on 20 September 1854. The 33 bus route to Kingstanding went from the City Centre by way of Summer Lane and Alma Street to Six Ways, Aston. When the Perry Barr tramway route was abandoned on New Year's Eve 1949, the 33 was diverted from the former route to get to Six Ways by way of Newtown Row. This view of 1719 (HOV 719), having just passed into Alma Street from Six Ways, with the Royal Exchange public house behind it, was taken on 15 December 1949, just a fortnight before the re-routing. By this time Alma Street had some pretty appalling back-to-

back courtyards such as Myrtle, Victoria, Builth and Roslin Places; despite their attractive names they were dingy and unhealthy brick-floored courtyards with communal outside lavatories and criss-crossed by washing lines. Parked on the left is a Middlesex-registered 1935 Chrysler DeLuxe Eight. *G. F. Douglas, courtesy of A. D. Packer*

1734 (HOV 734)

Middle Travelling along Broad Street is 1734 (HOV 734), one of Perry Barr garage's long-lived PD2s. This part of Birmingham was extensively regenerated as Birmingham's 'Golden Mile' in the 1990s, with the International Conference Centre, Symphony Hall, Centenary Square and Brindley Place replacing all the buildings in this 1966 view. The Brush-bodied Leylands were most attractive buses, with their wide radiators matched by the even wider cab windscreen. Latterly Perry Barr had the last 57, starting with 1699, and they remained at the Wellhead Lane premises until their withdrawal, the last ones going in October 1968. Perry Barr operated almost the whole of the long cross-city routes and 1734 is passing St Martin's Street as it approaches Five Ways working on the 7 route to Portland Road, where it will terminate in the narrow confines of Selsey Road on the Smethwick boundary. Following is an almost new 3574 (BON 574C), a 1966 Daimler 'Fleetline' CRG6LX with a Metro-Cammell body, working on the 12 route to Bartley Green. *R. F. Mack*

1751 (HOV 751)

Bottom Speeding along Finchley Road towards the terminus of the 33 bus route in about 1962 is 1751 (HOV 751). This route was introduced on 18 August 1930 from the City into the then developing Kingstanding Estate as far as Ellerton Road; subsequent housing developments allowed it to be extended along Finchley Road to the junction with Kings Road on 2 January 1933. The Kingstanding municipal housing estate had provided housing for more than 30,000 people by the previous year, and even included the opening of Birmingham's 30,000th council house by the Minister of Health, Arthur Greenwood. However, it was a bleak area, being both very

high up, exposed to cold northerly winds, and having very few amenities other than the main shopping centre at the Circle in Kingstanding Road. By the time 1751 headed along the by now tree-lined Finchley Road, it had received the small black fleet waistrail numbers that somehow seemed to lack the dignity of the old gold numbers and in bad weather were rendered illegible by the road mud. *A. Yates*

1756-1843 (HOV 756-843)
Daimler CVD6; Daimler CD6 8.6-litre engine; MCCW H30/24R body, es 3.1948-1.1949, w 1.1962-9.1964

These were the first buses to have the Daimler CD6 engine, developed during the war and trialled extensively in Birmingham with the seven wartime CWD6s. The comparatively short CD6 unit enabled the cab to be 6 inches shorter than the equivalent CVG6 body, so the platform was lengthened by 6 inches. However, the engine was more difficult to maintain and this accounts for their early withdrawal. The original intention was to award the body contract to Burlingham, but that firm's specification did not meet Birmingham's requirements. 1756-1788 were the last post-war buses to be fitted with a handrail across the front upper saloon windows. When new, 1843 was exhibited at the 1948 Commercial Motor Show and was fitted with the Brush body from 1715. 1822 was exhibited at the British Festival in Copenhagen, Denmark, between 30 August and 12 October 1948 and carried a plaque on the front bulkhead to commemorate this event.

1761 (HOV 761)
Below Three days after the Coronation on 2 June 1953 1761 (HOV 761) is still carrying its pair of Coronation flags, mounted on a specially made two-holed bracket just beneath the destination box. Operating on the 58C shortworking to Wagon Lane, Sheldon, it is pulling away from the stop outside Small Heath Post Office in Coventry Road, opposite Small Heath Park. Just to the right is a branch of A. D. Wimbush, one of the largest bakers and confectioners in Birmingham, while behind the bus is St Oswald's Road, with a branch of Wrenson's grocery store on the far corner. These buses were noted for their extremely quiet and sophisticated ride, which may be why Daimler-engined buses were allocated to Coventry Road garage to replace the 'silent service' of the trolleybuses. *Author's collection*

1779 (HOV 779)
Bottom The old Yardley trolleybus terminus continued to be used by the replacement motorbuses until the construction of the Swan Underpass began, finally opened during 1967. Pulling out of the former trolleybus turning circle is 1779 (HOV 779), with its handsome 54-seat MCCW body. It is operating on the 57B route, which went to the somewhat hidden terminus in Station Street alongside New Street Station's southern edge. This route had replaced the 93 trolleybus route, one of the two pioneer trolleybus services along Coventry Road to Yardley. The 93 and the replacement 57B both served Birmingham's wholesale markets area, but only ran on weekdays. Subsequent reductions in passenger numbers resulted in the 57B becoming one of the few bus routes to be closed, on 31 March 1961. *G. F. Douglas, courtesy of A. D. Packer*

1798 (HOV 798)
Opposite top Travelling along Pershore Road is 1798 (HOV 798), the first oddment of this batch of Daimler CVD6s. It is working on the 45B service, which replaced the former 36 route tram service to Cotteridge. After the trams were abandoned, the new bus service was extended to the City boundary at Alvechurch Road, West Heath, as the 45 bus route. The reason for the fitting of the almost wartime-style 'hit-and-miss' upper saloon front windows is lost in the mists of BCT's records, but it happened fairly early in the bus's career. This section of Pershore Road, which had originally been a turnpike road, was developed on the western side during the 1820s by

the Calthorpe Estate. Behind the city-bound Vauxhall Velox EIPV six-cylinder saloon are some of the large detached villas that were later additions to this part of Edgbaston. *R. F. Mack*

1803 (HOV 803)

Middle After just a year in service, 1803 (HOV 803) was re-introduced on 8 July 1949 with the proposed design for the triple indicator display boxes that was to be introduced on the 'New Look'-front buses whose delivery was to begin during the following year. As a result the bus spent the next few years wandering around various garages so that conducting crews could become familiar with the new design. It therefore always looked slightly peculiar, an 'odd bus out'. It is seen travelling out of the city centre in Hill Street, working on the 15B service to Garretts Green Lane in South Yardley. it has an old single-track destination blind in the lower box, suggesting that Liverpool Street garage did not have a suitable new-style blind in stock. Against the skyline is the gaunt iron framework of New Street Station, hit no fewer than six times between 16 October 1940 and 28 July 1942 by wartime enemy action. Such was the estimated cost of restoring the intact but time-expired framework, that the decision was made to pull it down. The demolition took more than 3½ years, suggesting that 1803 has only just been rebuilt and returned to service. *S. N. J. White*

1819 (HOV 819)

Bottom Working on the 60 service, 1819 (HOV 819) has just turned from the Bull Ring into Moor Street towards the end of 1960. This bus route to Cranes Park was never a trolleybus service, but was introduced on 1 July 1951 when the Coventry Road trolleybuses were abandoned. The bus is pulling away from the stop where, until only a few months before, the

early-19th-century premises of Oswald Bailey's Army & Navy Stores had stood. In the background are the remains of Charles Edge's imposing Market Hall, on the Bull Ring between Bell Street and Phillip Street; it was 365 feet long, 106 feet wide and could hold around 600 stalls, selling fresh fruit and vegetables, meat, poultry and fish. Its Bull Ring portico stands impressively awaiting its fate as Gallagher's demolition cranes prepare to reduce it to rubble. In the event they failed, and the solid old building had to be blown up, something that the Luftwaffe had failed to do in 1940. 1819 was always allocated to Coventry Road garage and was withdrawn at the end of September 1963. *Author's collection*

1844-1930 (HOV 844-1930)
Daimler CVG6; Gardner 6LW 8.4-litre engine; MCCW H30/24R body; es 12.1948-10.1949, w 6.1963-11.1968

The 87 buses of the 1949 batch of Daimler CVG6s were undoubtedly the stalwarts of the Inner Circle 8 route, around which they always seemed to be slogging their way. As with all but one of BCT's Daimlers, they were fitted with Wilson pre-selector gearboxes and fluid flywheels. 1852 was used for development work on the 'New Look' front, but was never in service with the concealed radiator. The long Gardner 6LW engine meant that the cab was longer in front of the driver's cab door, so in order to remain within the legal length of 26 feet the platform area was correspondingly 6 inches shorter than on the Daimler CVD6 chassis. They all tended to run hot and were nicknamed 'pot-boilers'. They were virtually the

same as the GOE-registered 1556-1630 class, although at 7tons 16cwt they were 1cwt heavier.

1845 (HOV 845)
Below Accelerating away from the impressive and genuinely weather-proof bus shelters in Harborne Road is 1845 (HOV 845), working on the busy Inner Circle 8 route with the Five Ways Clock in the distance, and already 14 years old. These buses had pre-selector gearboxes, which enabled the driver to change gear by just depressing the gear-change pedal, located where a normal clutch would be, thereby making his life considerably easier. Coupled to the Gardner 6LW 8.4-litre engine, these buses were admirably suited to the day-to-day toiling around the 10-mile-long Inner Circle bus route, which passed through areas of heavy industry, Victorian terraced and back-to-back housing. However, this section of the route was part of the prestigious Calthorpe Estate, a suburb that included some of the most expensive houses in Birmingham, many of which dated from the time of William IV. *F. W. York/R. F. Mack*

1857 (HOV 857)
Bottom The 36 bus service was operated by Highgate Road garage and was introduced on 21 September 1936, running between Station Street, alongside New Street Station, and Richmond Road, Stechford, taking a circuitous route by way of Sparkbrook, Sparkhill and Tyseley. The Tyseley section went through an industrial area with extremely heavy peak-time loadings, but as the section from the City Centre to Sparkbrook

was duplicated by numerous other Corporation bus routes, the decision was made to cut it back to Stoney Lane on 21 September 1958. 1857 (HOV 857) entered service on New Year's Day 1949 and worked for a month short of 20 years. When Highgate Road garage closed on 14 July 1962, this Daimler was transferred to Lea Hall garage. It is seen here in Stratford Road, Sparkbrook, during the last year that the 36 ran from the City Centre. It has just passed the garage of Smith's Imperial Coaches on the corner of Farm Road, while on the right is the notice board outside the premises of Lewis & Randall, the well-known commercial photographers, whose archive, now in the Local Studies Department of Birmingham Central Reference Library, dates back to the 1850s. *R. F. Mack*

inter-war period with a mixture of private and council houses on both sides of the River Cole flood plain; the valley itself was left as open and recreation land due to its frequent inundations. *R. F. Mack/BaMMOT*

1912 (HOV 912)

Top On a misty winter's day in about 1958, one of the industrious CVG6s, 1912 (HOV 912), pulls away from the stop in Hob Moor Road, working the 15B route to Garretts Green. It covered 594,000 miles in its long life, which, together with 1926, was the highest mileage achieved by any member of this class. These were very hard-worked buses, especially those like 1907 being operated by Liverpool Street garage, and were used on some of the city's most arduous routes such as the long cross-city 16 family of services between Garretts Green and Hamstead, of which the 17J was part, the Inner Circle 8, and the circuitous 28 route, which passed through eastern and northern suburban Birmingham. Hob Moor Road (hobgoblins supposedly haunted the surrounding woodland) was developed in the

1925 (HOV 925)

Above This bus has just entered Vaughton Street, having come from High Street, Deritend, by way of Alcester Street, and is at the junction with Thomas Street as it travels through the back streets of this inner-city area, which still had some of the worst slum housing in Birmingham. An example can just be seen on the right behind the Homepride lorry, an Atkinson flat-bed four-wheeler registered in Coventry in March 1949, making it just seven months older than the bus. 1925 was another of Liverpool Street garage's CVG6s, and it is working on the City Circle 19 route in about 1957, as it still sports trafficators. On the left is the White House public house, the only retail outlet in this part of Vaughton Street. *R. F. Mack*

1931-2030 (HOV 931-999/JOC 200/JOJ 1-30) Daimler CVD6; Daimler CD6 8.6-litre engine; MCCW H30/24R body; es 10.1949-2.1950; w 6.1964-9.1966

These were the same as the 1756-1843 class and were the last exposed-radiator Daimlers to be purchased. The 100 vehicles were ordered in 1947, and were 'rushed through' to be delivered as replacement vehicles for the Moseley Road tramcars. These handsome buses were extremely quiet and refined, although they perhaps lacked engine oil economy. They gave good service, particularly at Coventry Road and Perry Barr, where they operated on the long routes operated by those garages. 1933 was exhibited at the 1949 Commercial Motor Show.

1954 (HOV 954)

Below On 1 March 1951 the 48 route has been diverted away from its normal route into Moseley Village; it usually went by way of Salisbury Road, but because of road works both the 48 and the 1A service are having to use Park Hill, a tree-lined suburban road not normally used by buses.

Daimler CVD6 1954 (HOV 954) has just crossed the junction with Augusta Road and is on its way to Alcester Lanes End by way of the nearby Moseley Village. It is being followed by one of Acocks Green garage's AEC RT-type 'Regent IIIs', working on the 1A service. It was always something of a surprise that the 48 route should pass through some of the most pleasant areas of Edgbaston and Moseley, having reached them by way of Balsall Heath, which had some of the city's worst mid-19th-century slums. The route largely replaced the old 'Chinese Railway' tram routes through that run-down inner-city area, covering the former inbound 37 and 39 tram routes along Gooch Street and Longmore Street before following the inbound 39 tram route along Lincoln Street and Willows Road to the junction with Edgbaston Road opposite the north-eastern corner of Cannon Hill Park. 1954 was one of the first half of this batch of 100 exposed-radiator buses to enter service at Moseley Road garage on 2 October 1949. They replaced all the Moseley Road tramcars, and most, including 1954, spent their entire lives there until they were somewhat prematurely replaced by the second batch of Metro-Cammell Daimler 'Fleetlines' in the KOV-registered batch in June 1964. *A. D. Packer*

1972 (HOV 972)

Below left On 1 October 1950 the 55B bus route became the direct replacement for the Alum Rock 8 tram route, although it represented a considerable route extension when compared to the trams. As the 55 service it was extended as the new housing development moved outwards towards the city boundary. The first extension took place in 1951, a second occurred in 1953 and the final one, in 1963, took it to Kitsland Road, within walking distance of the shopping centre in Chester Road, Castle Bromwich. In about 1928 plans had been mooted for the 8 tram route to be extended from its terminus at the Pelham public house in Alum Rock Road, for which the Corporation had acquired all but the final Parliamentary approval to go along Burney Lane as far as Stechford Road. Even today along Burney Lane there are wide open grass spaces intended for the tram tracks that never materialised. When the new 55B bus service was introduced, it terminated at The Raven public house, which was then virtually the last completed building on the expanding post-war Shard End Estate. With The Raven in the background, and the junction with Bucklands End Lane in the distance,

1972 (HOV 972) waits at the bleak new terminus soon after being drafted in to Washwood Heath garage's bus fleet in October 1950 to replace the trams. *Author's collection*

1979 (HOV 979)

Top Speeding down Kingston Hill, Coventry Road, is 1979 (HOV 979), one of the neat-looking CVD6s allocated to Coventry Road garage, which was almost opposite the Kingston Cinema seen here in the background. The cinema opened on Sunday 4 August 1935 and closed as a cinema in 1968. It is showing a William Wyler film, *The Loudest Whisper*, which was released in 1961 and starred Audrey Hepburn, Shirley MacLaine and James Garner. This dates the photograph to about 1962, and shows how well the Corporation maintained its buses; they were always kept in immaculate condition, even though 1979 was to remain in service for barely another two years. It is travelling into the City on the 60 route with a full load of passengers bound for the Albert Street terminus, while behind is a Morris Minor saloon and an Austin F-type lorry. *Photofives*

2008 (JOJ 8)

Middle Judging by vehicle allocation records, 2008 (JOJ 8) was still one of Yardley Wood garage's Daimler CVD6s in 1958, though like 2009-2016, which had recently made the move to Acocks Green garage, it would soon join them as a single bus transfer. It is seen here in Woodthorpe Road, Kings Heath, at the junction with Brandwood Road, and is working on the long inter-urban 18 route between The Valley public house at Haunch Lane, Yardley Wood, and Ley Hill Farm, Northfield. This route had begun in March 1929 as a BCT service between The Green in Kings Norton, Cotteridge and the Bell public house in Northfield, although its origins were, most unusually for Birmingham, with an independent bus operator. The route was extended at both ends during 1930 and even spawned an extension from Kings Norton to Redhill Road, West Heath, which was given the new number 23. The original 18 route became the 18A in November 1930, when it was extended by way of the extremely steep Parsons Hill to the Kings Heath tram terminus before going via Taylor Road and Haunch Lane to the new terminus at The Valley. Much later, on 19 February 1956, the Ley Hill Farm extension in Northfield was instigated, and re-numbered 18. Behind the bus is a row of three-storey shops on the boundary of Brandwood Cemetery, whose entrance is in the distance marked by Harry L. Mark's monumental masons, just beyond the Esso petrol sign. The shops included a newsagent, a sweet shop, a greengrocer, a grocer, a chemist and, occupying the nearest premises, Fozards off-licence. *R. F. Mack*

2026 (JOJ 26)

Bottom The 25 route was originally a cross-city peak-hour service between Hall Green Station in Highfield Road and Finchley Road, Kingstanding, opening on 17 December 1934. It was effectively a 29 along Stratford Road across the City Centre and through Hockley, but once it reached Hawthorn Road on Kingstanding Road it followed the 33 service through the large crescents of the 1920s housing estate to the terminus at the junction with Kings Road. It was cut back on 5 October 1942 to run only from the City Centre to Kingstanding as part of the wartime economy drive, and was never reinstated. 2026 (JOJ 26), one of Perry Barr garage's exposed-radiator Daimler CVD6s, is entering Hockley Hill, having passed through Hockley Brook on its way into the City on the peak-hour-only 25 service. On the right is the cobbled entrance to New John Street West. It is being followed by a Morris Minor 1000 saloon and a rear-engined Renault Dauphine. On the left, beyond the speeding Ford Anglia 105E, is the Grand Turk public house on the corner of Icknield Street, along which the Inner Circle 8 bus service ran. *R. F. Mack/BaMMOT*

2031-2130 (JOJ 31-130)
Daimler CVD6 with 'New Look' concealed radiator; Daimler CD6 8.6-litre engine; MCCW H30/24R body; es 9.1950-8.1951, w 3.1965-10.1966

These were numerically the first buses in the fleet to be fitted with the Birmingham-styled 'New Look' front, as well as the first Daimlers to have the three-quarter-width bonnet. The term 'New Look' came from Christian Dior's long and curvaceous skirt length, which had been introduced into his Paris fashion salon in the spring of 1947. They also had the triple indicator destination display, which had been pioneered on exposed-radiator 1803. The MCCW bodies were based on the previous classes but with a slightly extended upper saloon, a straightened front and a windscreen profile that married up to the front profile and incorporated a recessed windscreen. The buses were numerically the first class to have sliding ventilators and, when new, as with all the 'New Look'-front

buses, were fitted with decorative wheel discs. They were ordered in 1947 and had a very protracted delivery time from the bodybuilders. 2033 was exhibited at the 1950 Commercial Motor Show.

2031 (JOJ 31)
Below The first bus in the class, which entered service on 20 September 1950, a full three weeks before the second, is passing Digbeth Civic Hall. With its trafficator arm extended, it is about to cross the tram tracks in Digbeth and turn right into Rea Street while working on the 50 route to the Maypole terminus, which was an extension of the Kings Heath tram route converted to buses only about a year earlier. The bus has the attractive set of wheel discs fitted to all the city's 'New Look' buses, giving the already well-thought-out design a certain extra 'classiness'. Behind the Daimler is trolleybus 68 (FOK 68), a MCCW-bodied Leyland TB working on the 94 route along Coventry Road to Sheldon, which dates this scene to no later than the last day of June 1951, when the trolleybuses were somewhat prematurely abandoned. *S. N. J. White*

2044 (JOJ 44)
Bottom The hoarding on Chilton's newsagent's headboard shows that the 'Confessions of Mr Teasy-Weasy', a flamboyant society hairdresser whose real name was Raymond Bessone, were making the more frivolous headlines during 1961. This was in the days just before wholesale demolition erased this part of Balsall Heath in the mid-1960s. 2044 (JOJ 44) is travelling along Cox Street West, where the cobbled sets of the roadway are broken by the tarmac laid

where the tram tracks of the inbound 37 and 39 tram routes used to be. On the extreme right is Upper Cox Street, with the round-fronted, three-storey off-licence owned by Mrs Florrie Shaylor. The bus is working on the 48 route towards Moseley and beyond to the terminus at the Maypole public house, which it shared with the 'main-line' Moseley Road 50 service. *R. F. Mack*

2114 (JOJ 114)

Right Fillery's Toffee was a popular confection, made in Birmingham at the company's National Works between the Wilder's Fireworks factory and the Brooke Tool works in

Warwick Road, Greet. As a result of this local connection, advertisements for the toffee were regularly carried on Birmingham's buses during the late 1950s. One of Perry Barr garage's CVD6s, 2114 (JOJ 114), turns from Addison Road into Alcester Road South, Kings Heath, when working on the outer ring of the Outer Circle route in about 1957. The right turn towards High Street was followed almost immediately by an acute left turn into Vicarage Road, making this section of the long 11 route particularly hard work for the driver, especially when he had a full load of passengers! Although the bus has by this time lost its wheel discs, it still retains its full-length front wings and trafficators, although by this time there had been a fad for painting the back of the arms cream in order to match the rest of the bus. In theory this worked, but at a distance it just made the already shorter first lower saloon bay look even shorter. *R. F. Mack/BaMMOT*

2122 (JOJ 122)

Below A Triumph Herald saloon, first registered in May 1960, overtakes 2122 (JOJ 122) in Witton Lane, followed by a former military Austin K3 3-ton lorry, one of 17,097 that emerged from the Longbridge Works between 1939 and the end of the war. On the left is the churchyard for the Parish Church of Aston, St Peter and St Paul. A church with the same name was mentioned in the Domesday Book, and although the fine 15th-century tower and spire remain, most of the church was rebuilt to the 14th-century-inspired designs of the well-known Victorian ecclesiastical architect J. A. Chatwin between 1879 and 1890. The bus is working on the 39 route from Martineau Street to Witton, passing through Aston Cross with its aromas from Ansells Brewery and Garton's HP Sauce factory. 2122 had a 15-year life with the Corporation and was one of the last of the batch to be withdrawn, on 31 October 1966. *A. Yates*

2131-2180 (JOJ 131-180)
Leyland 'Titan' PD2/1; Leyland 0.600
9.8-litre engine; Leyland H28/26R body;
es 3.1949-6.1949, w 7.1967-12.1968

These were standard Leyland-bodied Leyland 'Titan' PD2/1s bought virtually 'off the peg'. Unlike their pre-war equivalents they had the normal Leyland 'L'-shaped staircase, and were fitted with standard thin-backed Leyland seating, which in the lower saloon had a Leyland-patterned, rather than BCT, moquette. They were rushed into service to operate on the 2B route between Kings Heath, the University of Birmingham, the Queen Elizabeth Hospital and the Ivy Bush, since in Dads Lane, Kings Heath, there was a low bridge that would just accommodate them, being slightly lower than the standard BCT bus. When delivered, the middle blue livery band was

omitted in error on buses 2131-2153. The passenger capacity was reduced from the standard H30/26R layout in order to comply with the normal BCT seating requirements. It was rumoured that these buses were to be numbered 297-346 in the pre-war sequence. They spent their entire lives at Hockley garage.

2136 (JOJ 136)
Below The first 23 of this batch were delivered with the middle blue band reduced to a blue line covering the moulding between the saloons. 2136 (JOJ 136) is in Dawlish Road, Bournbrook, on 1 June 1949, having been in service for just over two months. It is working on the 2B route and is on its way to Kings Heath from the Ivy Bush public house in Hagley Road by way of the Queen Elizabeth Hospitals. It is parked opposite the original BCT accumulator tram depot, opened on 24 July 1890 and finally closed by the Corporation on 11 July 1927, when it was replaced by Selly Oak depot. J. Cull

2138 (JOJ 138)
Bottom A convoy of Hockley garage's Leyland-bodied PD2/1s travels into the city along Livery Street led by 2138 (JOJ 138), working on the Oxhill Road 70 service in about 1961. This service had formerly been the 26 tram route, though in accordance with bus replacement services it had been extended about half a mile from the junction with Rookery Road to the Uplands public house in order that the buses could have a suitable turning

circle. 2138 is about to cross Lionel Street and is running alongside the extensive brick viaduct which carried the former Great Western Railway's main line out of Snow Hill Station towards Wolverhampton until railway services were abandoned in March 1972. Today the viaduct has been revitalised and now carries the Midland Metro trams to Wolverhampton as well as the Jewellery Line trains. Livery Street was opened in 1745 and got its name from Swann's Riding Academy on the corner of Cornwall Street; in turn it gave its name to the well-known Birmingham expression, 'A face as long as Livery Street', meaning a miserable look. *R. F. Mack*

2140 (JOJ 140)

Top Probably the fastest double-decker buses in post-war fleet, with their excellent power-to-weight ratio, the Leyland-bodied PD2/1s spent their entire lives based at Hockley garage. Here they were employed on the cross-boundary services through West Bromwich, and the two longest cross-city services, of which the 16A was one. The date must therefore be before 7 December 1958, which was when the route reverted to its original number 16, as 2140 (JOJ 140) turns from Bromsgrove Street into Hurst Street, passing Legg's tent-making works and The Australian Bar public house, next to the A4167 road sign on the left. The bus has travelled into the city from Whittington Oval, Yardley, and is on its way to the Hamstead Road terminus in Hamstead just beyond Rocky Lane, just on the north side of the River Tame valley, marking the boundary with West Bromwich. *A. B. Cross*

2166 (JOJ 166)

Above The Soho Road bus route to the city boundary at West Bromwich Albion's Hawthorns ground was numbered 72 and was introduced on 2 April 1939 when the 23 tram route was abandoned. 2166 (JOJ 166), which entered service on 1 May 1949, passes through Hockley Brook about five years later, returning from the Hawthorns ground. It has just descended Soho Hill, where the large three-storey shops have their sunblinds pulled down. These were part of Hockley's late-Victorian shopping centre, which included the Birmingham Municipal Bank on the corner of Farm Street. The bus is about to pull away from the stop opposite Whitmore Street, the location of Hockley bus garage, built in 1888 as BCT's cable tram depot and finally closed in May 2005 as part of a regeneration of the Hockley Brook area. 2166 is standing roughly where the cable trams had to coast across the gap between the inner cables from Colmore Row to Hockley and the outer cables from Hockley Brook to the New Inns in Handsworth. *G. Burrows*

2170 (JOJ 170)

Leaving Springfield Road and negotiating the very tight traffic island in College Road in about 1958 is freshly

repainted 2170 (JOJ 170), working on a 29A service. The houses, Board Primary School and the solitary shop in College Road all dated from the last decade of the 19th

century and virtually marked the end of the city's pre-First World War expansion. Hockley-based 2170, the first of the class to be withdrawn, on 31 May 1967, has come from the Baldwins Lane terminus at the boundary with Shirley and will travel through Sparkhill on its way into the City Centre before heading off across the northern suburbs to Kingstanding and the Pheasey Estate in Aldridge. The 29A was the only Birmingham City Transport bus route that technically started and finished outside the Birmingham boundary. *R. F. Mack/BaMMOT*

2181-2230 (JOJ 181-230)
Leyland 'Titan' PD2/1; Leyland 0.600 9.8-litre engine; Park Royal H29/25R body; es 10.1949-3.1950, w 2.1965-11.1969

These 50 buses completed the order for 200 Leyland double-deckers. At 7ft 6in wide, they were the only PD2/1s ever to receive this style of Park Royal body, which was similar to that built on the AEC 'Regent' III RTs of 1947, but of five rather than four bay construction. The buses conformed to most of Birmingham's stringent interior requirements, but had a Park Royal-style L-shaped staircase. Although a non-standard body design, the resultant vehicle was an extremely handsome bus, spoiled perhaps by the almost wartime opening window at the front of the lower saloon in lieu of opening bulkhead hoppers.

The first 15 buses were delivered with the front destination box about 3 inches too high, and as a result the middle blue livery band above the cab was straight and did not dip beneath the route display. From bus 2196 the destination box was lowered and the blue livery band had a dip in it and a thinner centre section. This variation in livery roughly marked the division of their allocation, with usually about the first 14 buses being garaged at Hockley while the larger group were at Rosebery Street until its closure on 29 June 1968. 2184 was fitted with a Pneumocyclic gearbox in February 1958 and thus sounded more like a Leyland 'Atlantean', while 2204 was nominally owned by Bristol-Siddeley, who fitted it with their experimental automatic transmission system, though it never ran in revenue service in this form. One vehicle, 2229, was actually operated by WMPTE.

2186 (JOJ 186)

Left The cross-city 16 service travelled by way of New Street and Corporation Street before reaching its last central Birmingham bus stop under the commodious canopy outside Greys department store in Bull Street. The routes to Perry Common, Kingstanding and Pheasey, as well as this one to Hamstead, then crossed the junction with Colmore Row, at that time dominated by the distant large Boots the Chemist shop, before entering Snow Hill. The stop outside the side entrance steps to Snow Hill Station's booking hall, taxi ranks and platform entrances was only used by these bus services, and must have been the shortest distance in the City Centre between any two bus stops! The building on the right of this circa 1959 view was part of the Great Western Hotel, whose main entrance was on Colmore Row. This hotel was built in 1863 over the mouth of the 596-yard tunnel, and enlarged in 1871. 2186 (JOJ 186) was one of the first 15 buses bodied by Park Royal to have the destination boxes fitted too high up, which resulted in the middle blue band not dipping beneath the aperture. *R. F. Mack*

2190 (JOJ 190)

Right Waiting at the West Bromwich Corporation bus stop outside the Woodman public house (only demolished in 2004) in Holyhead Road, at the Birmingham-West Bromwich boundary, is attractive-looking 2190 (JOJ 190). Next to the telephone box is a Bundy Clock similar to the one on the opposite side of the main road. The slush left after the winter snow is in some ways appropriate, as just in front of the bus is West Bromwich Albion's Hawthorns ground, which, at 547' feet above sea level, makes it the highest Football League ground in England and Scotland. As the bus is not fitted with a Coronation flag holder, it must date this view to about 1951. 2190 entered service on 1 November 1950 and is working on the 74 service to West Bromwich and Dudley. As this was a joint operation between BCT and West Bromwich Corporation, there were operating conditions peculiar to this and the 75 service to Wednesbury. Most odd was that, here at the Woodman, passengers crossing the boundary in either direction had to rebook to continue their journey, a situation that lasted until 27 August 1967. M. *Rooum*

2206 (JOJ 206)

Below The 95 bus route to Ladywood followed that taken by the 33 tram service, which had terminated in Icknield Port Road. The replacement bus service was introduced on 31 August 1947, initially from Paradise Street in a strange arc-like route along Bath Row to cross Broad Street at Five Ways, then on to a new terminus in Northbrook Street at the junction with Dudley Road, barely 1½ miles from the City terminus. These Park Royal-bodied Leyland 'Titan' PD2/1s were synonymous with Rosebery Street garage, and at a maximum the garage had about the last 37 of them. 2206 (JOJ 206), one of those built with the destination box at the corrected lower height, is working into the City Centre along Bath Row in about 1963; it is passing the Accident Hospital, which had originally been opened as the Queens Hospital in 1841. A. *Yates*

2223 (JOJ 223)

Above The B81 service was only operated as a morning and evening peak-hour extra; it went to the top of Cape Hill, Smethwick, and turned back at Windmill Lane at the junction with Waterloo Road and Shireland Road. Emerging from beneath the Council House Extension Bridge in Edmund Street alongside Birmingham's Art Gallery is 2223 (JOJ 223), working on this infrequently operated route on 27 August 1967. As the Hillman Husky car turns into Victoria Square, the bus will turn right into Congreve Street towards Summer Row and Dudley Road. Beyond, 2210 (JOJ 210) is working on the B82 service to Bearwood and is picking up passengers from the substantial shelters in

Edmund Street, having been overtaken by 2223, another from the same batch. *Author's collection*

2228 (JOJ 228)

Below Bearwood's Bus Station was opened in February 1952, and though it was in Bearwood, which is outside Birmingham, the bus shelters behind the distant Morris Minor are located in Hagley Road West, across the boundary in the city. The bus, parked somewhat casually, is working on the B82 route, which was the direct successor to the 29 tram service, abandoned, together with the other 'main-line' Dudley Road routes, on 30 September 1939. The replacement bus services were numbered B80 to B87 and were all nominally jointly operated with BMMO, though in reality the Corporation only regularly operated the B80 to B83 services. This rear view of the Park Royal-bodied PD2/1 reveals the large entrance area of the platform, which is then restricted by the incursion of the L-shaped staircase. The buses had the standard Park Royal two-windowed upper saloon rear emergency exit, and it was a strange coincidence that all the Leylands in the Birmingham fleet, be they bodied by Brush, Leyland or Park Royal, all had this two-window layout, to the exclusion of all other post-war half-cab double-deckers. *P. Tizard*

2231-2260 (JOJ 231-260) Leyland 'Tiger' PS2/1; Leyland 0.600 9.8-litre engine; Weymann B34F body; es 6.1950-11.1950, w 9.1962-12.1971

Originally ordered as 35 PS2/1s to replace the 45 pre-war Daimler COG5 single-deckers, the order was amended to 30, with the balance arriving as the five 'Olympic' vehicles of the next class. The bodies were ordered from Weymann of Addlestone in Surrey instead of Metro-Cammell, who were their associate bodybuilding partners but who were unable at the time to construct single-deck bodies. The complete bus weighed 6tons 18cwt 1qtr, more than a pre-war Daimler COG5 double-decker, but coupled with the powerful Leyland 0.600 9.8-litre engine they were capable of being used as dual-purpose vehicles. Their saloons were finished in the usual BCT style with sliding ventilators, lots of wooden trim and the 'acanthus leaves and berries' pattern of moquette. They were the only exposed-radiator buses to have recessed windscreens and the 'New Look' triple indicator destination blinds (except for the experimental 1803). 2231-2236 had their side destination boxes mounted over the first bay, the remainder having the box over the second bay. 2231-2247 were fitted with saloon heaters in 1958, while 2260 was similarly equipped ten years later. Thirteen buses, 2232/4/7/46-7/9/52-3/56-60, were converted to OMO in 1966, which involved removing part of the front bulkhead.

2231 (JOJ 231)

Top To celebrate the Coronation of HM Queen Elizabeth II, Birmingham City Transport mounted a pair of small Union Jack flags on a specially made two-holed bracket. 2231 (JOJ 231), the first of the 30 attractive-looking Weymann-bodied PS2/1s, carries these flags just next to the word 'NORTHFIELD' on the destination blind. The bus is working on the 27 service in June 1953 and is travelling towards the suburban terminus in Kings Heath. It is picking up passengers at the stop in Cartland Road, with Pershore Road in the background and the Pavilion cinema across the open ground on the right. *S. N. J. White*

2245 (JOJ 245)

Above The driver has just manoeuvred his bus around a large Humber Super Snipe saloon, having just come through the low bridge beneath Northfield railway station in Church Hill; the station, whose entrance is to the right of the Humber, was opened on 1 September 1870, one of the last on the line to be completed. The 12ft 6in-high bridge, together with the even lower one on the same former Midland Railway line at Bournville, meant that the 27 route would always be operated by single-deckers. The route opened between Kings Heath and Hay Green on 2 October 1935, and had been extended via Northfield to West Heath on 5 July 1952, when the abandonment of the Bristol Road tram routes enabled the local bus services, including the single-deck-operated 23 route, to be rationalised. 2245 entered service on 4 August 1950 and was withdrawn in May 1969; today it is beautifully restored by the Acocks Green Preservation Group. *A. B. Cross*

2256 (JOJ 256)

Above The 35 route was introduced on 31 October 1965 to link the Brandwood Park and Allen's Croft housing estate with Kings Heath, about 2 miles away. 2256 (JOJ 256) is in Vicarage Road opposite the row of shops next to Kings Road in about 1967. The single-decker appears to be carrying a full standing load, while the driver waits to collect the fares from the two passengers who are about to board. This PS2/1 was converted to OMO in January 1967, which involved the fitting of an angled window between the driver's cab and the front bulkhead, part of which was removed, an electric ticket machine, and a swivelling driver's seat. Although the Corporation had purchased 24 single-decker Daimler 'Fleetlines' in 1965 and a total of 18 AEC 'Swifts', the number of single-deckers required in the city was growing and the conversion of some of the half-cab 'Tigers' was a most useful, albeit late, addition to the fleet strength. *R. F. Mack*

2259 (JOJ 259)

Below Early in their careers, quite often during summer weekends, the PS2s were hired in by Midland Red if they were short of coaches for a journey to London or excursions to Blackpool or Weston-super-Mare. These single-deckers, with their high-powered 9.8-litre engines and well-appointed interiors, were more than equal to their 'coach-timed' forays into the English countryside. Nearly 18 years later, in apparently the twilight of their careers, the Selly Oak garage-based PS2/1s were occasionally put to work on the 99 Limited Stop service to Rubery. This had been introduced on 3 April 1967 and was the domain of the Strachan-bodied Ford R192s, which entered service at the same time. 2259 (JOJ 259), an old-fashioned half-cab single-decker with a seating capacity of only 34 passengers – albeit sitting fairly comfortably – stands at the Suffolk Street end of Navigation Street in 1967 in front of 3657 (JOL 657E), which was one of the fast, lightweight 46-seater Fords. Rest assured that, even at this late stage of its career, the PS2/1 would give the Ford a good run for its money! *L. Mason*

2261-2265 (JOJ 261-265)
Leyland 'Olympic' HR40;
Leyland horizontal 0.600
9.8-litre engine; Weymann
B36F body; es 7.1950-
9.1950, w 4.1968-5.1968

This was the first underfloor-engine bus to be built by Leyland Motors. The first four were built by Metro-Cammell at Elmdon, the remainder by Weymann. A total of only 23 were built, and these five were the largest batch to be produced. These integral single-deckers were unusual in being only 27ft 6in long and 7ft 6in wide. They had their panels riveted into the frames and the floor line was marked with a decorative polished strip. The interior had aluminium-faced window cappings, but otherwise was completed to normal BCT standards. All were converted to OMO in the autumn of 1963 when the seating capacity was reduced to 34.

2261 (JOJ 261)
Above Birmingham Corporation began a bus service from Queen's Drive, between the old LNWR and MR sides of New Street Station, to Elmdon Airport terminal on 2 May 1949 using a pair of Daimler COG5s, 53 (AOP 53) and 38 (BOL 38). The City terminus was altered to a new City Air Terminal centre alongside Baskerville House in Easy Row, brought into operation in October 1951. The first of the five 'Olympics', 2261 (JOJ 261), entered service on 27 July 1950, some five weeks before the other four vehicles. Always known as the 'Airport Bus', it was placed on the Elmdon Airport service in October 1950 with a reduced seating capacity of 32, which allowed more passenger luggage to be carried. It is fairly full with passengers, while careful examination reveals that the back seats are unoccupied and taken up with luggage. It is leaving the Air Terminal and turning into Easy Row a few months after this new facility had been opened. *Author's collection*

2263 (JOJ 263)
Below In the latter part of their careers, the HR40s were used to open new OMO single-decker routes. On 1 December 1963 the new 4 route was opened from Cotteridge to Pool Farm Estate in the Primrose Hill area of Kings Norton, a distance of barely 2 miles. The first three of the class were converted to OMO in September 1963 and transferred to Yardley Wood garage, which operated the service. 2263 (JOJ 263) looks as though it is being kept busy as it loads up with passengers at the temporary bus stop in Pershore Road South outside Cotteridge Fire Station. The traffic island in the distance at the end of Middleton Hall Road, which the Austin Loadstar articulated oil tanker is negotiating, is where the 4 route turned around having come up the steep hill from Kings Norton. *Author*

2264 (JOJ 264)

Below When at Grammar School in the early 1960s, the author remembers playing Rugby Union on the playing fields laid out in the horse-racing in-field of Birmingham Racecourse at Bromford Bridge. This was the site of the city's racecourse until 21 June 1965, when, despite more than a century of horse-racing tradition, it was closed down and within two years was a huge municipal housing estate with a mixture of low-height and multi-storey buildings. The 26 route began operation from Highfield Road, Alum Rock, into the Bromford Bridge Estate on 11 September 1967, and simply ran the length of the estate's 'spine road' alongside the River Tame, which was just across the road on the left. Within a few years Bromford Drive would stand in

the shadow of the M6 Motorway. Waiting at the terminus of the newly introduced 26 service in Bromford Drive is 2264 (JOJ 264), with the turning-round point in the throat of Hyperion Road in the background. Driving these buses on a 'turn' was hard work, as fares had to be collected from passengers, and the driver also had an extremely awkward manual gearbox to operate, which made it possible to change upwards into reverse when trying to obtain third gear. *L. Mason*

2265 (JOJ 265)

Bottom The original 27 route went from Hay Green to Kings Heath and served the famous Cadbury's factory in Bournville. Unfortunately the adjacent Worcester & Birmingham Aqueduct and the railway bridge over Bournville Lane next to Bournville station had a height clearance of only 10 feet. With Roger Moore modelling for the Regular Army on the poster on the right, 2265 (JOJ 265) emerges from the dark recesses of the Bournville Lane aqueduct, having just left the chocolate-producing factory on 19 June 1952 while travelling to Stirchley and on to Kings Heath. The aqueduct and railway bridge marked a distinct boundary between George Cadbury's Bournville Garden Suburb Estate, begun in 1893 to the designs of W. Alexander Harvey, and the Victorian 'tunnel-back' housing of Stirchley, which was barely ten years older. *G. F. Douglas, courtesy of A. D. Packer*

2266-2395 (JOJ 266-395) Crossley DD42/6; Crossley HOE7/4B crossflow 8.6-litre engine; Crossley H30/24R body; es. 11.1949-5.1950, w 12.1963-9.1967

This order for a total of 260 Crossley DD42/6s was the largest post-war order placed with the company. By the time of their delivery Crossley Motors had been taken over by AEC, and the second half of the batch (2396-2525) benefited from the later, more efficient engine, although BCT had wanted this batch to have this new HOE7/5B engine, which did not enter quantity construction until April 1950. The

chassis had the new Crossley synchromesh gearbox. The Crossley bodies were built to the normal BCT designs and could be distinguished by having thinner corner pillars to the side of the upper saloon and a thin black line to separate the khaki roof paint from the cream paintwork of the rear dome. 2266-2304/2323-28 had Simms electrical and fuel pump systems. 2305-22/2329-95 had CAV electrical and fuel pump systems. 2266-2345 had half-drop saloon windows, while 2346-95 had sliding ventilators.

2269 (JOJ 269)

Above The short 39 service followed the route taken by the 3X tram route that it replaced on 1 January 1950. The terminus at Witton Square was outside CBT's Aston Manor tramcar depot; originally opened for steam trams, it was converted to electric operation on 6 October 1904 and finally closed as an operating Corporation tramcar depot on 31 December 1949; today it is the Aston Manor Road Transport Museum. On Wednesday 27 March 1957, 2269 (JOJ 269), which became the second of the class to be withdrawn, on 31 January 1964, after extensive platform damage, waits for passengers as its crew stand having a quick 'fag' before going back to the City by way of the aromatic delights of Aston Cross, courtesy of the malt of Ansells

Brewery and the vinegar from the HP Sauce factory. In the background, beneath the huge IMI factory and the Witton Arms public house, a Brush-bodied Leyland 'Titan' PD2/1 comes out of Witton Road while working on the cross-city 7 route to Portland Road. *Author's collection*

2296 (JOJ 296)

Below One of Miller Street garage's allocation, 2296 (JOJ 296), climbs the Walsall Road Bridge over the Birmingham Canal near Perry Barr Locks while working on the 51 service in Walsall Road on 8 September 1966. By this time, exposed-radiator Crossleys were being withdrawn virtually every month, but this bus was to survive for another year, to belong to the select 17 that were the last of the 130 of the type to be withdrawn at the end of September 1967. The Great Barr 51 service to the Scott Arms at the Birmingham boundary was taken over from Midland Red on 4 May 1958, replaced the latter's 119 service. This part of Walsall Road had been part of the somewhat desolate Perry Barr UDC before being absorbed by the predatory expansionist Birmingham in 1928. Fairly quickly Walsall Road became lined with 1930s semi-detached housing, while nearby the Beeches and Booth's Farm municipal housing estates were developed. *D. Johnson/Millbrook House*

2342 (JOJ 342)

Below The 26-mile long Outer Circle 11 route was also the preserve of exposed-radiator Crossleys, which were operated by Acocks Green, Harborne and Perry Barr garages. 2342 (JOJ 342) spent the whole of its life working from Acocks Green garage, and has just crossed the Six Ways junction in Erdington and entered Wood End Road when travelling towards Tyburn Road and Washwood Heath in July 1962. Going in the opposite direction is a Ford Consul EOTA bearing a registration from June 1955, which would not have found favour across the Atlantic! The attractive-looking Crossleys had an easier-to-manage synchromesh gearbox when compared to the Leyland

PD2/1s, and had excellent brakes, but their steering joints required regular greasing to avoid heavy steering. The sidedraught HOE7/4B 8.6-litre-engined buses were slightly underpowered as they had to pull 8tons 7cwt 1qtr of very solidly built bus. Despite these deficiencies, the class averaged over their lives between 460,000 and 480,000 miles, with 2342 surviving to be part of the mass withdrawal of Acocks Green's Crossleys at the end of February 1967. *D. F. Parker*

2346 (JOJ 346)

Bottom The first of the exposed-radiator Crossleys to have sliding ventilators, which had been pioneered on 1647, was 2346 (JOJ 346). Its sides were also tidied up, as there was now no need for any guttering over the saloon windows. 2346 is turning from Stephenson Street in front of the Queens Hotel into Navigation Street in August 1954 when working on the 34 service to the Hagley Road West terminus in Quinton. Behind the bus is the Midland Hotel block on the corner of Lower Temple Street, which formed part of Joseph Chamberlain's 1875 Improvement Scheme. Parked on the busy forecourt of New Street Station is a 1951 Standard Vanguard Phase I, unusually fitted with left-hand drive. Following the bus is a 1930s Rolls-Royce Phantom II. *G. F. Douglas, courtesy of A. D. Packer*

2364 (JOJ 364)

One of the many Crossley DD42/6s allocated to Perry Barr garage was 2364 (JOJ 364), seen here on the heavily loaded cross-city 29 service from Baldwins Lane, Hall Green, to Pheasey Estate, Aldridge, beyond Kingstanding Circle. It is in Digbeth in about 1965, not long after the route had been renumbered from 29A on 29 November 1964. By this date the bus had flashing indicators to replace the original trafficator arms, and the gold fleet numbers had been replaced by the small black fleet numbers on the waistrail. It is crossing the junction with Moat Row, with the premises of Smithfield Garage on the distant corner of Meriden Street, having left the previous stop outside Midland Red's Digbeth Coach Station.

Following the bus is one of the revolutionary 72-seater BMMO D9s, 5361 (6361HA), which is working into Birmingham's recently opened Bull Ring Bus Station on the 184 service from Dorridge, Bentley Heath and Solihull, then following the Corporation's 44 bus route along Warwick Road. *R. H. G. Simpson*

2396-2425 (JOJ 395)
Crossley DD42/6; Crossley HOE7/5B downdraught 8.6-litre engine; Crossley H30/24R body; es 1.1950-6.1950, w 11.1964-9.1967

This was the last class of Birmingham buses to have exposed radiators. They were also some of the first buses built by Crossley Motors to have the new HOE7/5B downdraught engine, and were mechanically identical to the next batch of 100 'New Look'-front buses, while their bodies were the same as 2346-95. Because of falling passenger numbers, 2403-2425 were withdrawn prematurely when their Certificates of Fitness expired, though strangely the earlier vehicles were among the last

exposed-radiator Crossleys to be withdrawn. This accounts for the wide range in the achieved mileage of these 30 buses, which was between 382,000 and 512,000 miles.

2411 (JOJ 411)

The bus was exactly one month old when it was seen in Washwood Heath Road on 4 June 1950. It is working on the 21 service, which covered the outer part of the 28 service, between Kingstanding and Bordesley Green East. This route number, together with the corresponding 22, which was the old tramcar route number to Bolton Road, and ceased to be used on 13 February 1955 when the complete bus route was renumbered 28A. On this sunny summer's day the passengers are queuing to get off the bus while a few more wait in the corrugated-roofed shelter to board the sparklingly painted Crossley. On the other side of the tramcar central reservation, next to the mock-Tudor Fox & Goose public house, both built in 1913 when the tram extension reached this terminus with Bromford Lane, is one of the earlier batch of crossflow-engined Crossleys, 2349 (JOJ 349). This bus was allocated to Perry Barr garage and is working on an Outer Circle shortworking. *T. J. Edgington*

2415 (JOJ 415)

Below Leaving Northfield on the 62 service to Rednal, the bus looks in fine fettle as it pulls away from the bus stop outside Northfield Swimming Baths while carrying an almost 'three-bell' load of passengers. By this time the route to the Lickey Hills, which in tramcar days had been the major local tourist carrier, was now carrying much of the workforce of the British Motor Corporation's Austin plant at Longbridge. Following the bus is a Humber Super Snipe I luxury saloon, while in the distance is a brand-new Daimler 'Fleetline' CRG6LX with a single-deck Marshall B37F body, which entered service during 1965, not long before 2415's withdrawal on 31 December. On the opposite side of Bristol Road South is the wonderful Black Horse public house. This was designed in 1929 by C. E. Bateman

for the Birmingham-based Davenport's Brewery in the style of a Tudor manor house and looks so genuine that today it has a Grade II listed status. *R. H. G. Simpson*

2417 (JOJ 417)

Bottom On a sunny day in June 1959, 2417 (JOJ 417) loads up with passengers in Fox Hollies Road at the bus stop beneath the tall lime trees just beyond the Olton Boulevard East junction. The Crossley is one of Harborne garage's buses, although within three years it would be allocated to Acocks Green garage, located in the distance at the junction with Summer Road. The bus driver is wearing his summer lightweight khaki uniform and will soon be looking into his cab mirror to see if the conductor is about to 'ring him off'. He will then gently squeeze the gear lever into first gear without revealing to the passengers, by 'crunching' the gear, that the bus has a 'proper' gearbox, albeit a very easy-to-operate synchromesh unit specially developed by Crossley Motors at the behest of Birmingham City Transport. The Crossleys 'had to be driven', and as a result, on a summer's day like this, they were harder work than the Guys or Daimlers, which had pre-selector gearboxes. Their steering was on the heavy side, but they had the best brakes in the fleet and for everyone except those sitting upstairs above the driver, where it always seemed very bouncy, they offered most comfortable ride of any Birmingham bus. *D. F. Parker*

2426-2525 (JOJ 426-525)
Crossley DD42/6; Crossley
HOE7/5B 8.6-litre engine;
Crossley H30/24R body;
es 2.1950-11.1950,
w 10.1963-11.1969

These 100 Crossleys were the first buses in Britain to be built with the 'New Look' style of concealed radiator (named after Christian Dior's 1947 skirt design) and three-quarter-width bonnet. The Corporation had seen how the Midland Red's concealed radiator could dramatically modernise the appearance of an otherwise normal half-cab double-deck chassis, so set about designing their own version. The development work was a joint venture between BCT and Guy Motors, which had begun in 1948 with a radical full-front design. Crossley Motors, whose order had been altered to include the modification of these last 100 buses to have the new concealed-radiator design, did very quick modifications to the existing exposed-radiator chassis. The result was that Crossley 'stole a march' on its competitors, and 2426 entered service more than three months before any 'New Look'-front vehicles. The buses had the HOE7/5B downdraught engine and Crossley synchromesh gearbox. The Crossley bodies were based on the previous exposed-radiator buses, but had an extended upper saloon, a straightened

front, a triple indicator destination display and a windscreen profile that married up to the front profile and incorporated a recessed windscreen. The buses had sliding ventilators and, when new, were fitted with decorative wheel discs. 2516 was exhibited at the 1950 Commercial Motor Show and spent six weeks at the 1951 Festival of Britain. These buses achieved some high mileages by BCT standards, with most falling between 440,000 and 580,000 miles, well in excess of that achieved by any of the Daimler CVD6 classes.

2426 (JOJ 426)

Top The first of the 'New Look'-front Crossleys was 2426 (JOJ 426), which entered service on 24 February 1950, more than three months before any other concealed-radiator Crossley and four months before the first 'New Look'-front Guy 'Arab' III Specials. 2426 was originally allocated to Acocks Green garage, to work on the 1A service that went past the General Manager's house in Wake Green Road. It was the only bus with a concealed radiator to have a step set into the nearside front wing, so that garage staff of smaller stature could see into the

radiator when it was refilled. In addition, together with show exhibit 2516, it had decorative chrome strips on the inside of the front wings and a different design of front wheel discs. It is standing outside the New Inns in Acocks Green Village in March 1950 alongside the impressive bus stop and the Bundy Clock. *R. T. Wilson*

2456 (JOJ 456)

Above The 'New Look'-front Crossleys operated on a large number of routes, and those allocated to Liverpool Street garage were frequent performers on the Inner Circle 8 service. 2456 (JOJ 456) is at the bottom of Lee Bank and is about to pass into Sun Street. In the background are the flats and maisonettes of the Lee Bank Comprehensive Redevelopment Scheme. The bus is carrying a full load as it negotiates the last stages of the rebuilding of the road in 1968 before it became part of Lee Bank Middleway, but with its shortened front wings (undertaken in order to get a better airflow over the front brakes) and the small black fleet numbers, it has only a few months left before its withdrawal at the end of July 1968. *M. R. Keeley*

2466 (JOJ 466)

Above Doctors, nurses and patients stand on the balconies of the General Hospital, at the bottom of Steelhouse Lane, in order to get a better view of the closure of the Birmingham tram system when the Erdington trio of services were replaced by buses. Tram 569 was the last 79 service tram to run to the Tyburn Road terminus at Pype Hayes, having left the Steelhouse Lane terminus at 10.35. A few minutes later, the first replacement 66 bus service to Pype Hayes followed, operated by 2466 (JOJ 466), which is overtaking a parked Austin A70 police car while on its way into Corporation Place. The bus is in immaculate condition but has lost its rear wheel trims. A nice touch was that 2465 worked on the first 65 service, but the plan did not quite work as the first bus on the Erdington 64 route was 2301, an exposed-radiator Crossley. *R. Knibbs*

2468 (JOJ 468)

Below Travelling into the City when working on the 42 service from New Oscott is 'New Look'-front 2468 (JOJ 468), new on 1 July 1950. It was delivered to Acocks Green garage, but was transferred to Miller Street garage in time for the final BCT tram conversions on the Erdington routes, and stayed there for the rest of its operational career. The 42 service had been introduced on 7 September 1958, replacing parts of the Midland Red 107 and 113 routes along College Road to the New Oscott boundary. Well into its middle years, 2468 is passing along Dale End, having turned from Stafford Street, which is at the end of the tall buildings in the background. It is 1961, as the newest car is the Ford Anglia 105E on the right, which dates from the July of that year. Behind the Commer Cob II van are the premises of A. R. Wood & Co, who made utensils for breadmakers such as A. D. Wimbush, Bradfords, Hawley and Scribbans. Next door to Wood's is Coates plumber's merchants, by this time becoming one of the minority of businesses still trading in Stafford Street, as building leases and compulsory purchase orders in the area began to sound the death knell for this once important thoroughfare. *R. F. Mack*

2489 (JOJ 489)

Opposite above On a sunny early afternoon in the summer of 1952,

2489 (JOJ 489) stands in Lordswood Road alongside the Kings Head public house; dating from 1905, it replaced a Georgian inn that had stood next to the old Hagley Road tollgate building. The bus is within sight of Bearwood's main shopping area while the crew wait for their leaving time and clock-in at the Bundy Clock. The bus, very solidly built at 8tons 6cwt 2qtrs, entered service on 1 July 1950 and remained in service until 31 March 1969, having spent most of its life at Harborne garage. It has been preserved in this condition by the 2489 Group, one of whom is the author of this book. This is one of the earliest photographs of this preserved Crossley in service. *G. Burrows*

2518 (JOJ 518)

Below The Yew Tree public house stood on the corner of Stoney Lane and Hob Moor Road, South Yardley. It was opened by Mitchells & Butlers on 22 January 1926 in mullioned Jacobean style when the housing development in the area had hardly begun. It looked as if it would last for years, yet it was closed on 26 July 2000 and demolished within the next three years to make way for a small shopping development. On a really miserable day in the mid-1950s, 2518 (JOJ 518) has left the distant bus shelter in Hob Moor Road and is following a 1934 Hillman Minx saloon past the Belisha beacon and across the zebra crossing in front of the pub. It is going to Garretts Green Lane on the 15B service, which means that the date is before the extension of the route to the Meadway, on 7 December 1958. It is fairly full with passengers, while the relaxed-looking driver obviously has the 'push-and-pull' method of steering a bus down to a fine art, judging by the position of his hands on the steering wheel. *R. F. Mack*

2526-2625 (JOJ 526-625)
Guy 'Arab' III Special; Gardner 6LW 8.4-litre engine; MCCW H30/24R body; es 7.1950-5.1951; w 1.1966-10.1977

After contractual problems with Leyland Motors and the impending demise of Crossley Motors as a chassis manufacturer, BCT began to look for an alternative chassis provider. Having wartime experience of the rugged Guy 'Arab' chassis, Birmingham turned to Guy Motors, which had not long before announced its new pre-selector option on the 'Arab' III, but with exposed radiators. As with Crossley, what Birmingham specified for its order for 100 26-foot-long Guy 'Arabs' was distinctly more than the standard vehicle manufactured at Fallings Park. To meet BCT's requirements, Guy's design staff produced a new basic chassis frame with a 16ft 4in wheelbase, no platform extension, new flexible engine mountings, and a Gardner 6LW engine coupled to a fluid flywheel and four-speed epicyclic pre-selector gearbox mounted amidships. So as not to infringe Daimler's patents, the gearchange lever was floor-mounted in the same position as a gear lever. Guy referred to the first 100 as 'Birmingham Arabs', but the Corporation had them down as 'Arab III Specials'! They were in reality a halfway house between the Mark III and Mark IV. A prototype 26-foot-long chassis, FD.70192, built in 1949, was used as a test bed and ran behind service buses in order to gain information; it was later returned to Guy Motors and broken up. While the chassis redesign work was taking place, in the spring of 1949 BCT and Guy developed a series of mock-up fronts, including a strange-looking full-fronted version. A sheet metal front with a blue-painted bonnet was also experimentally fitted to 1852 (HOV 852), a 1949 Daimler CVG6, in November 1948. This long front cowling was known as the 'New Look', after Christian Dior's radical early post-war skirt length, and the Guys had a more subtly curved shape than those built by Crossley or Daimler. The Metro-Cammell bodies were similar to their earlier post-war bodies but with a slightly extended upper saloon and a recessed windscreen profile that married up to the front profile and the by now standard triple indicator destination display. The buses had sliding saloon ventilators and, when new, as with all 'New Look'-front buses, were fitted with decorative wheel discs. From this point onwards all future half-cab buses had these features and gradually them term 'Birmingham Standard' was applied to all BCT concealed-radiator classes. These buses were very long-lived, with four lasting until the last day of ex-BCT rear-platform bus operation on 31 October 1977.

2541 (JOJ 541)
Below About to pass the showrooms of Patrick Motors, in Daimler House, Paradise Street, in 1951 is almost new 'Arab III Special' 2541 (JOJ 541). It has just left Victoria Square and has partly circled the Town Hall on its way out of the City Centre on the 6 service. It will turn right, then first left into Broad Street before travelling along Hagley Road until it branches off into Sandon Road. Its terminus will be outside the Birmingham Municipal Bank at the wide turning circle in the throat of Willow Avenue, about a 2-minute walk from Bearwood's shopping centre. The congested Paradise Street ran between Hill Street and the distant Suffolk Street and was first mentioned in 1792,

when it was improved from what had been little more than a track, to link with the main turnpike, opened in 1753, to Halesowen and Stourbridge. Trying to load up at their stands in Paradise Street are two Midland Red-owned, Brush-bodied BMMO D5s, the second of which, 3493 (MHA 493), is working on the 140 route to Dudley by way of Quinton and Blackheath. In front of those two buses is pre-war bus 915 (COH 915), working on the 48B service to Alcester Lanes End, Kings Heath. The rest of the vehicular traffic consists of a cross-section of the early post-war British car industry, with Morris, Hillman, Rover, Austin, Triumph and Ford cars, although just to the offside of the driver's cab of 2541 is a 1949 London CC-registered French-made Citroën Light 15. *Birmingham Central Reference Library, Local Studies Department*

2558 (JOJ 558)

Top right After Quinton garage was officially opened in October 1950, most of the first 40 of the solidly built 'short length' 'Arab III Specials', including 2558 (JOJ 558), were transferred there to replace Daimler CVG6s 1911-1930. The mud on the lower saloon panels rather hides the newness of the bus as it lets off its passengers at the bus stop outside the Hollybush public house in about 1951. The main bus route along Hagley Road and Hagley Road West was the 9, which went, as the rather

uninformative destination blind put it, to 'QUINTON'. This route was opened on 31 March 1919 to the Stag & Three Horseshoes public house at the top of Mucklow Hill, but was later cut back to the triangle made up of College Road and Ridgacre Road, just inside the Birmingham boundary. The Hollybush opened in 1937, effectively replacing the old Red Lion that stood on the same side of Hagley Road West but further up the hill in front of the bus. On the opposite side of the road, the parade of shops with flats above them are about a year away from completion. *Author's collection*

2586 (JOJ 586)

Above right The 44 bus service had its City terminus in High Street, so 2586 (JOJ 586) has just begun its run along Stratford and Warwick Road to Acocks Green in June 1967 as it travels along High Street. It had long been one of Acocks Green garage's buses, and by this late stage of its career had its front wings shortened in order to cool the

brakes, which were prone to fading. This bus entered service on 1 January 1951 and remained in service until the end of January 1972, having been inherited by WMPTE on 1 October 1969 and completing its career in the Black Country. Birmingham's High Street was first recorded in the 13th century as literally 'the high street', and during the 19th century it became important as shops started to replace market stalls as centres of retail trade. The site on the right was the headquarters of the Birmingham Co-operative Society, which stayed in this prestigious city centre site until 1 February 1985. Behind the Guy is the Marks & Spencer store, completed in 1955 to replace a previous 1920s building destroyed in an air-raid on 9 April 1941. For many years the City Council and the local bus operators had resisted the local traders' requests to make High Street traffic free, as increasingly it was reduced to little more than a bus station, and it was not until the end of 1998 that full pedestrianisation was achieved. *A. Yates*

2602 (JOJ 602)

Above The length of Vicarage Road was for many years the sole preserve of the Outer Circle route, which it first used on Wednesday 7 April 1926 when the final section of the route between the Kings Head and Acocks Green was first operated. The Kings Heath end of Vicarage Road around All Saint's Parish Church was lined with late-Victorian housing, which was really a continuation of the village. When the Outer Circle bus route first began, there was little else along the road other than open heathland, and about halfway along was The Priory, a grand late-Regency ivy-covered mansion owned by John Howard Cartland, the last of a family of brass-founders. 2602 (JOJ 602) has just left the stop near the junction with Kings Road at the western end of Vicarage Road when travelling towards Cotteridge in 1958. The Acocks Green garage-based bus is being operated on the 11 route along that part of Vicarage Road that had been developed in the 1920s. *R. F. Mack*

2617 (JOJ 617)

Below In June 1953 2617 (JOJ 617) waits alongside Warwickshire County Cricket Club's Edgbaston home in Edgbaston Road opposite the Tally Ho Grounds. Working on the 1A route and travelling towards Moseley Village, it is fitted with the tasteful pair of Coronation flags mounted below the front destination box. The Corporation's buses had begun to carry advertisements only two months earlier in order to gain revenue, as the advertising contracts on the tramcars were about to expire; 2617 has one for Littlewoods Football Pools. *S. N. J. White*

2626-2775 (JOJ 626-775) Daimler CVD6; Daimler CD6 8.6-litre engine; MCCW H30/24R body; es 7.1951-5.1952; w 2.1968-11.1971

This class of 150 buses broke new ground in a number of ways. The Daimler CD6 engine was an upgraded one sometimes known as the Mark VIII, though this was the last order from BCT to specify the quiet but more expensive to maintain Daimler engine. These buses were the first in the fleet to be 27 feet long, the extra length being used to enlarge the platform area. 2661 was delivered as H30/25R, with a double seat under the straight staircase on the offside of the lower saloon, and acted as a prototype for all future BCT 'Standards'. All previous Birmingham metal-framed body orders had the bodies built in two halves, but these buses were the first 'standard' BCT design to have one-piece metal-framed bodywork. This tidied up the side of the buses, removing the between-decks guttering, while the depth of the windows in each saloon was increased. It also had a curved lower saloon bulkhead window behind the bonnet, so designed that small boys could watch the road and the driver without having to sit on their mum's lap!

2633 (JOJ 633)

Top The replacement bus route for the 94 trolleybus was the 58, which began operation on 1 July 1951. The trolleybus overhead is still in place as 2633 (JOJ 633) passes through Hay Mills, within about a week of the 'silent service' abandonment; the trolleybuses were partially replaced by the first 30 of these Daimlers, operating from Coventry Road garage. The buses had slightly longer bodies than the trolleybuses but still with a seating capacity of only 54. They looked extremely smart with their slightly deeper saloon windows and the silver-and-black-painted wheel discs. Standing in Hay Mills near Kings Road, the bus looks positively gleaming as it works the 58 route. The new one-piece body could be easily identified because it lacked the moulded guttering between the decks just below the middle blue livery band. *D. Griffiths*

2654 (JOJ 654)

Above The top end of the Bull Ring above Moor Street was in fact High Street, and it was here, after the wartime bombing that destroyed the original retail premises, that a number of temporary shops were constructed on the site. These buildings survived until the late 1950s, when work on the original Bull Ring Shopping Centre and St Martin's Circus began. On the right is Woodley's house furniture store, and on the left is the Bull Ring Café, a sandwich bar owned by Leo Devoti that for the 1950s actually made a good cup of coffee! The bus standing on the stone sets of this steep part of High Street in late 1953 is 2654 (JOJ 654), from Coventry Road garage, and is working on the 60 route to Cranes Park Estate. This was introduced as a new route when the Coventry Road trolleybus routes were abandoned; it turned left at the Wheatsheaf public house, whereas the Lode Lane trolleybus route, which was never replaced, turned right towards Solihull and the Land Rover factory. *A. B. Cross*

2692 (JOJ 692)

Above After the withdrawal of some of the early post-war stock of buses, many garages had a large stock of single-track destination blinds. So that damaged blinds could be replaced, the good single-track blinds were commonly put into buses with triple indicator destination displays, producing a somewhat odd display of two sets of route numbers. 2692 (JOJ 692) turns from Stafford Street into the temporary Priory Street in about 1964 when this part of Birmingham was being redeveloped as part of the Inner Ring Road scheme. With its small black waistrail fleet number and shortened front wings, it is working on the 52 route, which went to the late inter-war municipal housing on the Beeches Estate off Walsall Road, replacing the former Midland Red 188 route on 1 September 1957. *Author's collection*

2727 (JOJ 727)

Below From their introduction in 1951 and 1952, Washwood Heath garage maintained about 20 of the smooth-running Daimler CVD6s. 2727 (JOJ 727), which spent the first 11 years of its life working with that garage's allocation of long-length Guy 'Arab' IVs and exposed-radiator Crossleys, speeds over the cobbles and the tarred-over tram-tracks in James Watt Street in about 1961 when working on an inbound 55 service from Shard End Estate, which will terminate in Old Square. From this angle the curved bottom of the front bulkhead window is visible, as are the two pull-in ventilators for the lower saloon, a feature, instigated in 1929 with the first of the Brush-bodied AEC 'Regents', that would end with this class of bus. *R. F. Mack*

2767 (JOJ 767)

Rosebery Street garage had the last 20 of the CVD6s, but because the buses did not have a B in the first route aperture, they always had to use a single-track display in the destination blind in order to show the route number. 2767 (JOJ 767) is in Heath Street. working on the B83 route in about 1963. This route had replaced the 31 tram route to Soho Station on 30 September 1939, and, after turning off Dudley Road, ran the length of the back-to-back and terrace-lined Heath Street before terminating at the Smethwick boundary. It was always operated by Corporation buses from Rosebery Street garage, whose allocation of 'New Look'-front Daimler CVD6s, which entered service between December 1951 and March 1952, ran very low total mileages, rarely reaching 380,000 miles. 2767 would survive until March 1971, having been taken over by the WMPTE. *A. D. Broughall*

2776-2900 (JOJ 776-900) Daimler CVG6; Gardner 6LW 8.4-litre engine; Crossley H30/25R body; es 7.1952-7.1953, w 1.1971-10.1977

This was the first half of an order for 250 Crossley-bodied Daimler CVG6s, and surprisingly they were the first CVG6s to be delivered since the exposed-radiator HOV-registered batch. These JOJ-registered buses took exactly 12 months to be delivered. Following the experiment with 2661, their seating capacity was increased by having a double seat beneath the staircase, thus becoming H30/25R.

2851 was fitted with a Daimatic gearbox in March 1957. After an accident, 2847 was fitted with electric doors, becoming H30/25RD, and saloon heaters in December 1959. 2799 and 2880 were fitted with Manchester-style glass-fibre fronts, in April and February 1958 respectively. All the buses in the class were taken over by the WMPTE in October 1969.

2782 (JOJ 782)

A somewhat dirty Daimler performs its duty during a dusty day in the summer of 1954. 2782 (JOJ 782) entered service on 1 July 1952 and was one of 38 placed into service in time to replace the Bristol Road and Cotteridge tramcars. By 1954 this bus was allocated to Liverpool Street garage, which operated the long 28A route, although by 13 February 1955 the through route was renumbered 28. It is pulling away from the row of Birmingham Co-operative Society shops in Hawthorn Road, Kingstanding, and behind it, on the corner of Charlton Road, is the late-1920s municipal housing that so characterised this part of Birmingham. *A. Yates*

2799 (JOJ 799)

Below As a result of accident damage, two of this class of Daimler CVG6s were fitted with a newly developed type of concealed radiator. Originally developed to the requirements of Manchester Corporation to improve the driver's nearside view, this arrangement became the standard front fitted to almost all the subsequent CVG series buses. 2799 (JOJ 799) is about to be overtaken by an Austin A30 saloon as it pulls away from the bus stop outside the offices of the Canadian Pacific Railway in Victoria Square, not long after receiving this new type of front. Painted all-over blue, the new glass-fibre front sat rather uncomfortably on the two buses that received them. 2799 is working on the 15A service to Whittington Oval, South Yardley, while behind it,

crossing the junction with Waterloo Street, is 2363 (JOJ 363), one of Perry Barr garage's many exposed-radiator Crossley-bodied Crossley DD42/6s. *R. F. Mack*

2829 (JOJ 829)

Bottom On Wednesday 13 May 1959, 2829 (JOJ 829) turns into Woodcock Street, whose claim to fame was its short section of dual carriageway that ran between Victorian three-storey back-to-back housing and Birmingham's second municipal Public Baths, which opened in 1860 to cater for residents of the surrounded houses who had no washing facilities. The bus is working on what would appear to be a well-patronised 99 service, except for the fact that generally it wasn't! The 99 was a Limited Stop service to Tile Cross,

which, except for the first section out of the City Centre by way of James Watt Street, Coleshill Street and Woodcock Street, followed the existing 14 service. Unfortunately, even in the 1950s, the traffic congestion was sufficiently bad that any advantage the bus had in only stopping at strategic points along the route was quickly, or slowly, nullified by the inability to keep to the time of even the existing 14 service. It began on 16 February 1959 and was discontinued just three months later, only two days before 2829's driver hauls the Daimler from the distant Ashted Row, where the early-19th-century shops include Nicholas Leslie's hairdressers and Gladys Bickley's tobacconist shop, all destined to disappear within the next ten years when the area was swept away for redevelopment. *B. W. Ware*

2833, 2828, 2044 (JOJ 833, 828, 44)

Top Even Birmingham's buses had to have an occasional holiday, and so it was that the two Crossley-bodied Daimler CVG6s 2833 and 2828 took their older distant auntie, Metro-Cammell-bodied Daimler CVD6, for a day out. The girls all went together to the riverside canal town of Stourport-on-Severn, where they stopped for a picnic alongside the canal basin on a lovely piece of soft grass, which tickled their tyres a lot as they didn't have many opportunities to sit on grass... They could see the big river, which was crossed by the long bridge that started almost in front of them, and were very glad that they didn't

have to wade across it as it was both wide and deep. From their vantage point they could see the Bridge Inn at the very end of the main street, where lots of people walked up and down buying food, drinks and souvenirs. One little boy even offered the three girls some of his ice-cream, but they declined by dipping and flashing their headlights at him. Eventually they had to go home, so they said bye-bye to Laurence the Launch and went home after having a lovely day out. *Birmingham Central Reference Library*

2847 (JOJ 847)

Above The most distinctive of all Birmingham's 'Standard' buses built between 1950 and 1954 were always those that had been altered in some way, and the perhaps the most distinctive was 2847 (JOJ 847). It was involved in an accident and was sent to Midland Red's Carlyle Road

Works, where the rear area was completely re-styled with an enclosed platform and electrically operated doors. The bus also received a Cave-Brown-Cave heating system and yellow-painted ceilings, and re-entered service on 10 December 1959. The bus spent most of its rebuilt BCT career allocated to Cotteridge garage, the entrance to which is on the right; it is leaving the bus stop in Pershore Road that was located where, until 5 July 1952, the 36 tram route terminated. It is working on the 45 service to West Heath and is directly opposite Watford Road, with George Mason's grocers and provisions shop behind the Bedford A5 tipper lorry on the left. 2847's conversion, which added almost 3cwt, looked very neat from the rear, but the frame did not match up with the nearside curvature of the body, so had a somewhat ungainly look from certain angles. *L. Mason*

2856 (JOJ 856)

Above The 14 route working is being worked by one of Birmingham's most unusual experimental buses. 2856 (JOJ 856), from Lea Hall garage, pulls away from a stop in Kitts Green Road during 1958. At first sight it looks like any other Crossley-bodies Daimler CVG6s from the 1952-53 batch, but closer investigation reveals that the front and rear wings are wider in order to accommodate 8-foot-wide axles. Additionally, 2856 has acquired extra-wide front wheel nut guard rings to ensure that the width of the bus 'on the road' is genuinely 6 inches wider than the otherwise unaltered Crossley body. This experiment was undertaken during 1958 in order to test the possibility of operating 8-foot-wide

buses, and although it did spend a lot of time without passengers, 'shadowing' service buses, in this case the mother and daughter have just alighted from it. Towards the end of the test period 2856 acquired shortened front wings in order to improve the airflow over the front brakes, thereby acting as a prototype for the rest of the 'New Look'-front bus fleet. *Author's collection*

2889 (JOJ 889)

Below The Bristol Road tram routes closed on 5 July 1952, and the replacement buses, allocated to Selly Oak garage, had originally included some of the brand-new Crossley-bodied Daimler CVG6s as well as the first of the 2901 class

of 27-foot-long Guy 'Arab' IVs. The new Daimlers were re-deployed fairly quickly, the majority being transferred to Liverpool Street although a few moved to Highgate Road. In April 1953 one of the last of the 2776-2900 class to be delivered, 2889 (JOJ 889), this time new to Highgate Road, is working on that dreaded Birmingham City Transport route 'SERVICE EXTRA', and is standing on the abandoned tram lines at Rednal terminus waiting for passengers who have been enjoying a springtime visit to the Lickey Hills, which still called for extra buses working 'foreigners' for Selly Oak. To the right are the gardens and the end section of the old Rednal tram shelters in the by now silent tramcar terminus loop. *Author's collection*

99 (LRW 377)
Daimler 'Freeline' G6HS;
Gardner 6HLW horizontal
8.4-litre engine; Duple
B30+30D body; b 1951

Daimler's answer to the Leyland 'Royal Tiger' and AEC 'Regal' IV was the 'Freeline'. LRW 377 was numerically the second 'Freeline' chassis to be built, with the chassis number 25001. The chassis was completed in April 1951 and was sent to Duple, where it received a bus body with a standee layout in Edinburgh Corporation livery and to their specification, with a rear entrance and a front exit, both having electrically operated doors as well as forced ventilation. LRW 377 was demonstrated to BCT between 29 March and 29 May 1952.

99 (LRW 377)
During the two-month trial that Birmingham gave to this prototype 'Freeline', the bus seems to have been exclusively operated on the long 28 route. This ran between Station Street in the City Centre to Great Barr by way of practically every suburb on the eastern and northern sides of Birmingham. On its way back to the Station Street terminus during April 1952, it seems 'loaded to the gunwales' as it pulls out of Oldknow Road, Small Heath, where its driver has just 'pegged the clock', and turns into Waverley Road alongside the BSA factory gates. That was the problem with the 'Freeline', as it had only 30 seats arranged in a 2-and-1 split, which allowed for nominally 30 standing passengers, whereas behind the Daimler the 'old-fashioned' Crossley DD42/6, which was only 18 months older, carried 54 passengers who were all seated. The 28 route, rather like the 36 route 25 years later, was deemed suited to this experiment of high-peak-time traffic and a low suburban ridership during the off peak. Unfortunately, at rush hour, although it had a capacity of 60, half of the passengers stood, while out of the peak, when the route had more heavily laden shoppers than workers, there were not enough seats! *Author's collection*

OTD 301
Leyland 'Tiger Cub'
PSUC1/1; Leyland 0.350
horizontal 5.7-litre
engine; Weymann
'Hermes' B44F body;
b 1952

This was one of the first pair of prototypes of the new lightweight 'Tiger Cub' chassis. It had a constant-mesh gearbox with air brakes and a neat-looking Weymann body, but within a year the body was fitted to a new chassis, numbered 520001, re-registered as RTB 49 and sent on its way as a demonstrator again. Its appearance

between 1 and 16 December 1952 was therefore one of its comparatively rare outings in this guise.

OTD 301
The 'On Hire' sticker in the nearside windscreen reveals that OTD 301 is being trialled by the City Transport Department. The single-decker is standing by the impressive bus shelters in Church Road, Northfield, on what looks like a bleak day in December 1952. It is working on the 27 service; having travelled from West Heath to Northfield, it will progress to Bournville and Stirchley before arriving at the terminus in All Saint's Road, Kings Heath. The bus might have been better received had there been a need by the undertaking for new single-deckers in the early 1950s. However, its lightweight construction, coupled to the small engine – which, after all, was why the 'Tiger Cub' model was developed in the first place – would have counted against it in Birmingham. Additionally, the 'Tiger Cub' was initially only offered with a constant-mesh gearbox, which since the wartime Guy 'Arab' IIs and a solitary Brush-bodied Leyland had not been a feature of any BCT buses. *Author's collection*

2901-3000 (JOJ 901-999, LOG 300)
Guy 'Arab' IV; Gardner 6LW 8.4-litre
engine; MCCW H30/25R body; es 7.1952-
3.1953, w 3.1966-10.1977

This was the first half of an order for 201 27-foot-long Metro-Cammell-bodied Guy 'Arab' IVs. Like the previous class of MCCW-bodied Daimler CVD6s, these had bodies constructed in one unit. All but the last six had the usual floor-mounted Wilson pre-selector gearbox, while those last six, 2995-3000, were built with David Brown constant-mesh gearboxes and were allocated together, as drivers from, briefly, Acocks Green and latterly Washwood Heath garage did battle with the gears. All but one of the class survived into WMPTE ownership. 2926 was rebuilt with a two-landing staircase and reseated to H32/25R in 1956, while 2982 and 2983 had twin sets of rear direction and stop lights fitted in the late 1950s after the Construction & Use Regulations changed for rear lights on new double-deckers. 2926/67-70/98-99 were all fitted with Auster opening ventilators in all three front-facing saloon windows.

2902 (JOJ 902)

Below The electricity supply has only been turned off for about 24 hours following the final tram, lightweight car 842, negotiating Navigation Street on Sunday 6 July 1952, the day after the last service trams. Selly Oak, which was both a tram depot and bus garage, had an allocation of 112

trams and these were replaced by a large number of the first of the new Crossley-bodied Daimler CVG6s and the first 20 of this class of Guy 'Arab' IVs. 2902 (JOJ 902) stands alongside the tall advertising hoardings in Navigation Street when working on the 63 service to Rubery, which replaced the 71 tram route. The rear view of the bus shows the large rear fleet numbers that were discontinued during 1953 when small numbers were substituted to allow the positioning of advertisements on the lower rear panelling. The last bus to be delivered with the larger rear numbers was 2968. Standing in front of 2902 is Daimler CVG6 2781 (JOJ 781), working on the 62 service to Rednal. The Daimler appears to have quite extensive accident damage to the panelling between the decks. There are subtle differences between the two bodies, the most noticeable being that between the khaki and the cream on the MCCW one there was a cream-painted body strap, whereas the Crossley body, with its one-piece rear dome, just had a black-painted line to separate the two colours. *R. T. Wilson*

2926 (JOJ 926)

Bottom Not long after its alteration in July 1956 to an H32/25R seating layout, 2926 (JOJ 926) stands at the 66 terminus in Eachelhurst Road, having turned round at the junction with Hansons Bridge Road, which was just a matter of yards from the city boundary with Sutton Coldfield. The conversion of 2926 involved the replacement of the straight staircase with a much steeper two-landing one, which resulted in the omission of the small stair window and a large blank panel on the off-side rear. Perhaps surprisingly, the triangular window over the rear wheels was retained. In addition, the bus received a full set of Auster opening front windows while, uniquely in the fleet, the sliding saloon windows were replaced by pull-in ventilators that each had wind deflectors. *A. B. Cross*

2953 (JOJ 953)

Opposite top A large number of the JOJ-registered Guy 'Arab' IVs were allocated to Selly Oak garage from new, until replaced by Daimler 'Fleetlines' during 1967. 2953 (JOJ 953) was one of them, and is seen operating on the 62 service in Bristol Street in about 1957. These splendid buses were well-suited to the Bristol Road's fast running, though their brakes were their Achilles' heel, as they were prone to fading during hot weather, a problem that plagued all the BCT Guys throughout their early years. As a result the front wings were shortened, losing the symmetry of the 'New Look'-front design, although the wings of 2953 have yet to receive this

treatment. By this time the trafficators had been replaced by the first design of indicators, which were long amber covers that gave a more subtle light than the later flashing units fitted in the 1960s. 2953 is waiting at the traffic lights at St Luke's Road with an Austin FX3 taxi alongside it. *R. H. G. Simpson*

2993 (JOJ 993)

Middle Many of the later-numbered Guy 'Arab' IVs, 2970-94, spent most of their BCT lives allocated to Acocks Green garage, and 2993 (JOJ 993) was no exception. It is in Warwick Road, Tyseley, just beyond Acocks Green Congregational Church in Stockfield Road, and is working on the 44 service to Lincoln Road North in about 1964. The church was consecrated on 20 June 1860 and had closed in 1956 to become the Warwick Road City Temple. 2993 was one of the last of the class to enter service, not appearing until 25 March 1953, by which time it had been given the small black waistrail fleet numbers and the second style of flashing indicator cover, but still retained its full-length front wings. Acocks Green garage's drivers seemed either to love or hate the Guys, and if one was unfortunate to be driven by one who hated them, the gear changes were positively thumped home, resulting in the front end of the bus seemingly lifting several inches and the poor conductor being thrown backwards as he tried to maintain his balance and still collect the fares! *A. D. Broughall*

3000 (LOG 300)

Bottom They looked the same, but they sounded different and required a lot of skill to handle their unforgiving David Brown constant-mesh gearboxes. 2995-3000 were delivered well in advance of their numerical position, arriving during the delivery of 2966-2973. The first four entered service on 1 December 1952, while the last two, including 3000, which had, for the class, the odd registration LOG 300, came on 1 January 1953. They were fitted with a normal gear lever, which was floor mounted like the gear selector lever, but in order to differentiate between the two the constant-mesh buses had red knobs on the gear levers. In addition, all six had a notice in the cab: 'WARNING. GEARBOX NOT

PRE-SELECTOR. ORDINARY TYPE CLUTCH AND GEARBOX'. 3000 is only a few months old as its driver prepares to pull away from the City Centre pick-up stop in Cambridge Street and is almost full of Birmingham City football fans on their way to St Andrews. *Author's collection*

3001 (LOG 301)
Guy 'Arab' IV; Gardner 6LW 8.4-litre engine; Saunders-Roe H30/25R body; es 11.1952, w 7.1972

This was the first of three experimental lightweight buses to enter service. The Corporation became interested in reducing costs and, rather like the rest of the British bus industry, began to realise that many of the buses in production were over-engineered and very heavy. Guy Motors was approached to produce a lightweight chassis, but was not prepared to make a one-off. What the firm did was to take out of the production line of the JOJ batch of 'Arab' IVs a normal production chassis that was modified by fitting lighter components. The Saunders-Roe body, built at Beaumaris, Anglesey, had a single lightweight floor/ceiling unit between the saloons linked to the main body frames, aluminium window and bulkhead cappings and lighter seat frames, and lacked the upper saloon guttering above the windows; it could be distinguished from the front by the slightly more prominent front route destination box. The whole bus weighed 7tons 4½cwt, about 17cwt lighter than normal. 3001 was exhibited at the 1952 Commercial Motor Show prior to entering service with a Gardner 6LW engine, but this proved to have too great a power-to-weight ratio and a Gardner 5LW engine was fitted in June 1953.

3001 (LOG 301)
This bus had the chassis number FD.71259, which would have placed it around 2960 in the previous class of MCCW-

bodied Guy 'Arab' IVs. From the outside its Saunders-Roe body was a remarkably good copy of the Birmingham product, and firm was well in the running to obtain the body contract for the MOF-registered Guy 'Arab' IVs, but for a variety of reasons, including not being able to meet the delivery date for all 100 bodies, the contract was awarded to MCCW. 3001 is in Victoria Square and has just crossed the junction with Waterloo Street. It is about to be overtaken by a Ford V8 Pilot as it loads up with passengers outside the offices of the Canadian Pacific Railway, who always had a splendid large-scale model of one of their ocean-going ships in the window. It is working on the 31A service to Gospel Lane while in original condition, including running with its original Gardner 6LW 8.4-litre engine. This was taken out and replaced by a 5LW 7.0-litre engine, reconditioned from a pre-war Daimler COG5, in June 1953. The unique body, on which Saunders-Roe must have spent a small fortune in development costs, lasted for almost 20 years, always operating from Acocks Green garage. *Author's collection*

3002 (LOG 302)
Daimler CLG5; Gardner 5LW 7.0-litre engine; MCCW H30/25R body; es 10.1954, w 7.1972

Only two Daimler CLG5s were ever bodied, this one and REH 500, which had chassis number 18334 and became Potteries 500. 3002 was the second of these two genuinely lightweight chassis and was fitted with a Metro-Cammell body that was a cross between the previous 'Aurora' body and the 'Orion', which was about to go into production. The complete bus weighed 6¼ tons with aluminium-covered interior window-cappings and bulkheads, lightweight seats and windows mounted in rubber rather than the standard window frames. A unique feature was the sliding cab door, which somehow added

a touch of modernity to an otherwise somewhat austere appearance.

3002 (LOG 302)
The bus is travelling into the City Centre in Bradford Street in about 1961, working on the 31A service. From the front it looked little different from the more usual BCT 'tin front' double-decker, except for the rubber-mounted front windows and the pair of slatted lower saloon front bulkhead air-ducts that replaced the more subtle normal type. 3002 has acquired the small black fleet numbers but has managed to retain, albeit temporarily, its full-length front wings. Like its lightweight twin 3001, it was allocated to Acocks Green garage throughout its 18-year career. The same-depth windows in each saloon gave it an airy look, but although it had all the accoutrements of a Birmingham bus, its black-rubber-mounted windows made it stand out as something different. Its body was prone to drumming, and in its early years was stiffened to remedy the problem. Following it is one of Moseley Road garage's MCCW-bodied Daimler CVD6s, 1964 (HOV 964), which looks positively antiquated by comparison. Had BCT required further buses after the 1954 deliveries, a slightly heavier 8-foot-wide version of 3002 might have been the result, but the three lightweight buses were to be just as much a cul-de-sac as Birmingham's last two tramcars, 842 and 843, which ironically enough were also lightweight! *R. F. Mack*

3003-3102 (MOF 3-102)
Guy 'Arab' IV; Gardner
6LW 8.4-litre engine;
MCCW H30/25R body;
es 5.1953-10.1954,
w 1.1971-10.1977

This was the second half of the order of 27-foot-long Guy 'Arab' IVs with the usual floor-mounted Wilson pre-selector gearbox. The original intention was to have these 100 buses bodied by Saunders-Roe, which had done such a good job with the lightweight 3001, but the company could not deliver the buses required by BCT, so the contract went to Metro-Cammell, which produced another batch of identical bodies. All the class passed into WMPTE ownership on 1 October 1969.

3004 (MOF 4)

Above The new MOF-registered Guy 'Arab' IVs were delivered in time to be in service on 4 July 1953 to replace the last tramcars in Birmingham when the Erdington group of routes at Miller Street depot were abandoned. Only 3003/4/5/7/8 entered service before this, on 1 May 1953, when all five were dispatched to Quinton garage to operate the 3A, 6 and 9 services. As a result they were the only buses in the class to actually carry Coronation flags in service; some, up to 3020, were fitted with the bracket, but were not in service in time to carry the flags. Within a few days of entering service, 3004 (MOF 4) is working on the 9 service in Hagley Road West heading towards Quinton, just beyond the Bass House pub on the corner of Wolverhampton Road South. *B. W. Ware*

3029 (MOF 29)

Below Two months later, 3029 (MOF 29) was one of the new buses placed into service to replace the Miller Street tramcars. On Friday 3 July 1953 it has been brought out of storage in Miller Street PW yard ready for the final take-over of the three Erdington tram routes the following morning. Strictly speaking, then, 3029 is not a 'Birmingham Bus at Work', but a 'Birmingham Bus Before It Ever Began Work'! The tram on the right is car 679, which would operate briefly on 4 July to Short Heath. In the entrance to the now emptying tramcar sheds is 2778 (JOJ 778), one of the 1952 Daimler CVG6s with Crossley bodywork. The final change-over on the Saturday from tram to bus began some time after 10.15am, and by midday the 2 tram to Erdington was the 64 bus service, the 78 tram to Short Heath was the 65 bus, and the 79 tram route to Pype Hayes was the 66 bus. *D. Caton*

3060 (MOF 60)

Top This is something of a mischievous photograph of a 'Birmingham Bus at Work'. 3060 (MOF 60) is working on the 11 route on a dreich day in January 1954 – the cheat is that this is not Birmingham's famous Outer Circle, but the one in Glasgow! Standing at the Yoker terminus stands of the 11 service is the Birmingham bus when it was being

demonstrated together with a Daimler CVG6 with a Crossley body, 3132 (MOF 132). They were all operated by Knightswood garage, which was primarily a garage operating mainly AEC 'Regents'. *J. Thomson*

3068 (MOF 68)

Middle This bus entered service on 1 February 1954 from Quinton garage, but then spent seven years working from the nearby Harborne garage until moving on once again in 1966 to Selly Oak. Therefore during its 15-year career it was based at three garages within a radius of 2 miles of each other. While at Harborne it was a frequent performer on the 21 service; this was introduced on 21 July 1957 and travelled along Bristol Road to just beyond Selly Oak before turning into Weoley Castle Road, thence via Weoley Castle Square across Barnes Hill to the Bangham Pit Estate terminus at Genners Lane, within site of Bartley Green Reservoir. In about 1962 the bus is turning into John Bright Street from Navigation Street, with Finlays tobacconist kiosk, set into the railway bridge wall, on the left. On the right 1935 (HOV 935), one of Moseley Road's many MCCW-bodied Daimler CVD6s, begins the climb up the steep Hill Street, where the columns of the City Museum & Art Gallery are visible. *R. H. G. Simpson*

3098 (MOF 98)

Bottom One of the last five of the class to enter service, on 1 October 1954, 3098 (MOF 98) turns into Edmund Street from Easy Row, with the impressive Baskerville House and the Hall of Memory in Broad Street serving as a backdrop. These impressive municipal buildings had been part of the intended Civic Centre, but were never completed due to the outbreak of the Second World War. The bus is working on the 3 service, the Ridgacre Lane terminus of which was about 200 yards short of Quinton bus garage. It is 1963 and by this date its front wings have been shortened. Within a few years all the buildings on the right as well as this part of Edmund Street would be swept away by the construction of the Paradise Circus section of the Inner Ring Road. *A. Yates*

3103 (MOF 103)
Daimler CVG6; Gardner
6LW 8.4-litre engine;
Crossley H30/25R body;
es 6.1954, w 12.1971

This was the third lightweight-bodied bus, but was the most standard of the three, having just a lighter version of the standard Crossley body. It weighed 7tons 4cwt, which made it comparable to 3001, but still 9cwt heavier than 3002. It had Auster pull-in ventilators in the upper saloon front windows and was the only body to have side ventilators in the rear dome side windows. The body had riveted panels, aluminium-covered interior window cappings and lightweight seat frames, yet still retained twin-skinned interior domes. The chassis number, 18173, would have placed it as 3112 had it received a normal Crossley body, but due to its lighter components it was delivered some 11 months after the next chassis number had entered service.

3103 (MOF 103)
One of the most important industrial sites in Birmingham belonged to Joseph Lucas, whose huge factory was built in Great King Street between 1889 and 1892. Here the firm manufactured acetylene, oil and electric lamps and, early

in the 20th century, diversified into, initially, cycle lamps, then car batteries, brakes, vehicle lighting systems, ignition systems, plastic components and eventually aerospace products. The 69 bus route replaced the 24 tram route on 2 April 1939 and went from Colmore Row to Lozells by way of Great Hampton Row and Wheeler Street, passing close to the Lucas factory; because of the latter's needs, it was diverted into Great King Street on 2 March 1964. Not long afterwards 3103 (MOF 103) travels along Great King Street working on the 69 route from Lozells, passing the derelict land where once stood time-expired 19th-century properties. In the late 1980s the Lucas empire began to collapse and with it went the seemingly impregnable Great King Street factory, which stands behind 3103. *R. F. Mack*

3104-3227 (MOF 104-227)
Daimler CVG6; Gardner 6LW 8.4-litre
engine; Crossley H30/25R body;
es 7.1953-10.1954, w 3.1966-10.1977

This was the second half of the order for 125 Crossley-bodied Daimler CVG6s, though many of them were stored for three months or more until most of the last of the pre-war buses were withdrawn. Numerically the first of the batch was lightweight 3103. These 27-foot-long buses were the same as the 2776 class of 1952. 3132 was used as a demonstrator to Coventry City Transport (December 1953) and Glasgow Corporation (January 1954), while 3201 was demonstrated to Chesterfield Corporation. 3163-3172 had fluorescent front destination lights. 3188 gained fluorescent saloon lighting and yellow-painted ceilings in November 1960. 3189 was fitted with a Gardner 6LX 10.45-litre engines between January 1959 and June 1971.

3149 (MOF 149)
The radiator grills of the 'New Look'-front buses tended to become the first thing to be damaged either in accidents in service or within the confines of the garage. As a result a simple fibre-glass mesh grill was created at Tyburn Road in 1964, this very plain front being pioneered by Crossley 2505. In about 1968 3149 (MOF 149) rattles its way over the cobbles and patched road surface of Suffolk Street, having just left the terminus at the top of the hill near Paradise Street. Devoid of any chromework and only

adorned with a BCT transfer, and with shortened front wings, the once neatly balanced design has been reduced to an economical yet totally unattractive appearance. It is on the 49 service to Kings Heath by way of the 1 in 13 climb up Leopold Street, which in the days of the 39 tram was the preserve of the 50 401 class four-wheelers, which had special air and oil brakes that made it impossible for them to run out of control. Fortunately 3149 had no need for such a braking system! To the right, behind the advertising hoardings, is the huge Central Goods Station, originally built by the Midland Railway. *A. J. Douglas*

3155 (MOF 155)

Top In 1964 3155 (MOF 155) speeds along Lichfield Road on the 65 service. Entering service on 1 November 1953 from Hockley garage, it was the last of these CVG6s to enter service for four months, as there was insufficient work to justify placing new buses in service. As a result, the next nine buses, 3165-3169, were placed in store in Witton tram depot and eventually entered service on 1 March 1954. This bus was moved to Miller Street garage when BCT took over the Walsall Road, Beeches Estate and New Oscott services from Midland Red, and spent seven years there. It is overtaking a June 1964-registered Ford Corsair 120E, parked outside Newbury's carpet and furniture store, as it approaches Aston Cross on its way into the City. Within 12 months 3155 would be on its travels again, to Moseley Road garage to replace the last of the 2031 class 'New Look'-front Daimler CVD6s. *J. Cockshott*

3186 (MOF 186)

Middle Entering service on 1 June 1954 and allocated to Perry Barr garage, 3186 (MOF 186) pulls up to the 5A bus stand in Snow Hill when still fairly new; it still has wheel trims and trafficators, and has acquired an advertisement for Hovis bread with butter in the days when 'bread and marg' was more commonly eaten. The one-piece Crossley body was built to a more restrictive price than that on the earlier 'tin-front' Crossleys, and at 7tons 19cwt was slightly more than 1cwt lighter than the equivalent MCCW Guy 'Arab' IV and 7cwt less than the Crossleys! Nevertheless, it was a good-looking Birmingham bus and, despite the rumour that the MCCW bodies were more durable, while the spares situation for the Guys was 'not good', the prospect of body swaps, with Daimler CVG6s receiving ex-Guy Metro-Cammell bodies, never materialised. *R. F. Mack*

3216 (MOF 216)

Bottom The climb up the Bull Ring was always a struggle, especially if the bus was fully loaded. The advantage of having buses with fluid flywheels and Wilson pre-selector gearboxes was that gear changes were almost impossible to miss, so on this steep climb the driver of heavily laden 3216 (MOF 216) must have been relieved that he wasn't driving a Leyland PD2/1, where he would have had the choice of pulling away and staying in first gear or changing down and in the process losing most of his road speed on this very slow change of gear ratios. The Daimler has just pulled away from the bus stop alongside St Martin's Parish Church while working on the cross-city 29A service to Pheasey Estate, Kingstanding, in about 1963. Originally, before the Inner Ring Road was built, the buses climbed straight up the hill to New Street, but by this time they had a much easier, though more circuitous, route around the newly constructed St Martin's Circus to the next stop outside the ABC New Street. *T. J. Edgington*

3.
1955-1962
YEARS OF TRIAL AND ERROR

The last of the Crossley-bodied Daimler CVG6s and Metro-Cammell-bodied Guy 'Arab' IVs entered service on 1 October 1954, while the last of the pre-war COG5s and Leyland 'Titan' TD6cs survived into the early months of 1955. Between 1955 and 1962 Birmingham City Transport only took on to its strength some 22 new buses, yet the contrast between the last new 'Standard' buses of 1954 and the new buses resulting from the events in these intervening years could not have been more marked! Initially there was no need for the Corporation to purchase new buses as the whole fleet between numbers 1481 and 3227 was only between one and eight years old. A new garage, the last as it turned out, was opened at Crossfield Road, Lea Hall, on 19 April 1955, completing three new purpose-built garages, the others being Yardley Wood (1938) and Quinton (1950), all of which were intended to open between 1938 and about 1942. The Transport Department was still reducing the Birmingham City Council Rates, with the Inner Circle, Outer Circle, 12, 14, 15 and 16, 29A, 45 and 61, 62 and 63 all showing healthy profits.

Unfortunately the storm clouds were, in 1955, beginning to gather on the horizon, with passenger numbers dropping alarmingly for the first time. This was due to the start of a major change in the social habits of the population, not just in Birmingham but across the country. The end of rationing, the availability of new cars on the home market and the new-fangled television meant that fewer people were using the buses during the day and also in the evenings. As a result certain peak-time services were reduced, and straight away buses became idle and revenue was lost even quicker than before. In addition, wage demands from both the traffic and engineering departments made it necessary for a series of almost annual increases in the price of tickets. The contemporary comic duo of Michael Flanders and Donald Swann summed it up in their song 'A Transport of Delight':

'...So cut down all the stages,
And stick up all the fares.
If tickets cost a pound apiece
Why should you make a fuss?
It's worth it just to ride inside
That thirty-foot-long by ten-foot-wide [!]...'

It was realised, however, that at some point the next generation of buses should be prepared for, and between 1955 and 1960 almost every chassis manufacturer courted Birmingham with offers to either examine new models or test new buses. It is known that a number of buses, not detailed in this book because they never operated in service, were seen briefly parked outside the entrance to the Transport Department in Congreve Street during this period: these include NTF 9, the solitary Leyland 'Titan' PD2/15 of 1952 vintage, which was still demonstrating its RTL-type gearbox in 1955 despite having a body built by Leyland, who had stopped bus-bodybuilding in 1954; PHP 220, also in 1955, a Daimler CVG6 with a lightweight 61-seat Northern Counties body; and 46 LTB in 1959, a slightly earlier Leyland 'Atlantean' PDR1/1 than the subsequently purchased 460 MTE. The latter vehicle was destined to receive three registrations in three different countries in the British Isles, which at the time was some sort of obscure record for a bus! Finally, two Roe-bodied Guy 'Wulfrunian' FDWs were examined, initially the first of the type to be built, West Riding's OHL 863, then the second demonstrator, 7800 DA, which amazingly, in view of the problems that later befell this advanced but problematical bus, had 78 seats. Undoubtedly there were other manufacturers' products that stayed in the city for a few hours, but again were not used in service or directly tested on the road.

The running of demonstrators was always done by specially selected drivers working from Lea Hall on the long, busy and arduous 14 group of services between Old Square and Tile Cross by way of Saltley, Alum Rock and Stechford. Initially the buses were 27 feet long by 8 feet wide, and briefly it seemed as though BCT, which had belatedly warmed to the idea of a standard bus being 8 feet wide, might be interested in buses of these dimensions. It had operated the four Daimler COG6s intended for Johannesburg between 1942 and 1954, although they were not allowed into the City Centre, officially at least, until 1947, and BCT had been given powers to operate 8-foot-wide buses since 11 February 1946.

Between 1955 and 1961 nine demonstrators were operated on the 14 Tile Cross service, and during that six-year period the size of the buses increased, the entrance position moved from the rear to the front, and finally the engine moved from the front to the rear. In the first category were two Park Royal-bodied AEC 'Regent' Vs, registered 88 CMV and 159 JHX, followed by a low-height Willowbrook-bodied Daimler CVG6, registered SDU 711.

The change in policy came when ACV Sales offered Birmingham an extended trial with the second Crossley 'Bridgemaster' to be built, registered 9 JML. This low-height, integral front-engined bus with a manual gearbox was never going to be the future of bus operation in the city, but it was 30 feet long and 8 feet wide, and had 72 seats and an open-back platform. The Transport Committee was keen to see how the conducting staff would cope with carrying their leather money satchels and Ultimate ticket machines on a fully loaded bus. The immediate reaction was that the Union representing the conducting staff 'blacked' the bus and refused to work it with standing passengers in the lower saloon. Without hesitation the Traffic Manager agreed to this request and, when large-capacity buses of these dimensions were purchased initially in 1961, they were never operated with standing passengers! 9

JML was purchased in August 1957 and was given the fleet number 3228.

The second bus built to the newly introduced Construction & Use maximum dimensions was VKV 99, a 74-seater Daimler CVG6/30, with a rear-entrance open-platform Willowbrook body, which in 1958 became the last new bus to operate in Birmingham with this layout. In 1960 there was another 'last', when AEC 'Bridgemaster' 2211 MK arrived. Although mechanically similar to 9 JML, it was the first bus to operate in Birmingham with a forward entrance since 94 (BOP 94), the unique 1936-vintage Metro-Cammell-bodied Daimler COG5. Although 2211 MK was the last new half-cab bus to be operated, it sounded the death knell for the traditional double-decker. This bus was briefly given the fleet number 3229 towards the end of its 11-month stay, but was returned to ACV and sold to Osborne of Tollesbury, Essex.

During this period, the Corporation brought back into service 41 pre-war Daimler COG5s, overhauled and repainted, in order to provide a float of vehicles for when three routes were taken over from Midland Red. The Transport Committee had wanted to have blue and cream Corporation buses running on all the main roads leading out of the city, but both the Aldridge Road and Walsall Road areas were not taken into Birmingham until 1929, by which time the Birmingham & Midland Motor Omnibus Company was well entrenched on these two arterial roads. Originally there was to be one more pre-war bus, but 1133 (CVP 233), with an English Electric body intended for Manchester, was discovered to have a cracked chassis and spent the next six years parked at the rear of Coventry Road yard as that garage's snowplough. In June 1957, by way of something of an anachronism, just before 9 JML was purchased the first of the revived Daimler COG5s, 1082 (CVP 182), came back on to the road.

On 1 September 1957, only months after problems with fuel rationing caused by the Suez Crisis, the service to Beeches Estate, numbered 52, was introduced. On 4 May 1958 the 51 service to Great Barr along Walsall Road commenced, then finally the third route to be taken over from Midland Red was the 42 service to New Oscott,

1082 (CVP 182)
The first of the 41 Daimler COG5s to be returned to service in 1957 was 1082 (CVP 182). Looking immaculate save for its unpolished radiator, the 20-year-old bus has just unloaded its passengers in Livery Street when working on a SERVICE EXTRA route from Handsworth. The bus will shortly follow the Park Royal-bodied Leyland PD2/1 around the corner in order to load up again outside the entrance to Snow Hill Station. *A. B. Cross*

first operated on 7 September 1958. One month later, in October 1958, something of a revolution took place at Tyburn Road Works. Due to a continuing long-standing shortage of skilled painters, the age-old practice of brush-painting gave way to spray-painting in two purpose-built spray booths, although the result was still *sans pareil!*

The next demonstration bus arrived in July 1960 and looked really 'modern', with a front entrance forward of the set-back front axle and a seating capacity of 72. This was 8072 DA, a prototype Guy 'Wulfrunian' FDW. The bus had a front engine, but with the untried all-round disc brakes and independent suspension, as well as having unbelievably heavy steering, the design had been insufficiently developed, and was quickly returned to Fallings Park, Wolverhampton.

It was during this period, on 5 July 1960 to be precise, that a BCT publicity officer had a moment of poetic inspiration and coined the advertisement that appeared on hundreds of Birmingham's buses on the between-decks rear panel. Hardly Shakespearian in its meter, it read:

'TO AVOID THE RUSH FOR A CAR
   PARK SPACE
TAKE A BUS TO ANY PLACE'

The bus that really showed the way forward was a Leyland 'Atlantean' PDR1/1 (460 MTE). This was the first rear-engined bus to be used as a demonstrator; it arrived in February 1960 and made a sufficiently good impression, particularly after being fitted with the larger Leyland 0.680 11.1-litre engine. It was later bought in May 1961 and given the fleet number 3230. Its success resulted in a further ten buses being purchased to test against the broadly similar Daimler 'Fleetline' chassis. These were numbered 3231-3240 (231-240 DOC) and were put into service on the short

43 service to Nechells and the 96 route to Lodge Road, Winson Green.

The first 'Fleetline' to be constructed was 7000 HP, and after being exhibited at the 1960 Commercial Motor Show in BCT livery, it was duly brought to Lea Hall garage and gave its first demonstration in a blizzard. Immediately fitted with a Gardner 6LX engine, 7000 HP, another candidate for the fleet number 3229, was quickly returned to Daimler and was replaced by an order for ten pre-production prototype 'Fleetlines' numbered 3241-3250 (241-250 DOC). These were then tested alongside the 'Atlanteans' on the same 43 and 96 routes as the prototypes for the next generation of buses.

By the start of 1962 the fleet strength, which had been stable at 1,822 only four years ago, was down to 1,719 buses, with the first of the post-war Daimler CVA6s and CVG6s having been withdrawn as surplus to requirements. Unlike the situation with pre-war buses and wartime buses 12 years earlier, very few of the post-war buses were ever sold for re-use. The ideas about larger buses and the concept of replacing ten older buses with nine larger-capacity vehicles came to a head when the reliability and fuel and maintenance economy figures were examined and the Daimler 'Fleetline' came out as the vehicle to be ordered. As if to prove that the 'sleeping giant' was awake again, BCT promptly ordered 300, with the body contract split 50/50 between Metro-Cammell and Park Royal for delivery over the following three years, and the die was cast until the end of Corporation bus operation in 1969.

88 CMV
AEC 'Regent' V MD3RV; AEC AV 470 7.685-litre engine; Park Royal H33/28R body; b 9.1954

This was the first AEC 'Regent' V to be built, being completed for exhibition at the 1954 CMS as a Crossley 'Regent' V with the chassis number CMD3RV.001, although originally it had the chassis number U.168623 in the experimental series. The MD series of 'Regent' Vs were a lightweight chassis and 88 CMV carried an attractive 8-foot-wide four-bay Park Royal medium-weight body. Demonstrated to BCT between 25 March and 15 April 1955, it was subsequently sold to OK Motor Services, Bishop Auckland, in May 1957.

88 CMV

The green-and-cream-painted 88 CMV was in Birmingham for only three weeks and, like all the vehicles demonstrated to the undertaking, was allocated to Lea Hall garage. The 14 service to Tile Cross Estate was used for all the vehicle trials, being considered as the one that combined all the Corporation's service characteristics. The attractively proportioned bus is in Burney Lane, travelling out of the City towards Stechford Lane. This was the first of three 27-foot-long demonstrators to be trialled, but within a year new legislation enabled the first 30-foot-long demonstration chassis to be put into service, whose higher seating capacity meant that the shorter demonstrators would not succeed in obtaining orders from BCT. *A. Yates*

159 JHX
AEC 'Regent' V MD3RV;
AEC AV 470 7.685-litre
engine; Park Royal
H37/28R body; b 6.1956

This was ACV's first attempt to get a major order from BCT. The bus was operated in a version of the Birmingham livery, and had the triple indicator destination display. Originally it had a four-speed synchromesh gearbox, but prior to its third visit the chassis was fitted with a 'Monocontrol' air-operated epicyclic gearbox, thus becoming a MD2RV chassis. It was subsequently sold to R. Chisnell, 'King Alfred', Winchester, in September 1958. It was demonstrated to BCT between 26 June and 21 July 1956, returning during January 1957. It returned with a 'Monocontrol' gearbox between 18 March and April 1957.

159 JHX

AEC really tried to get an order from Birmingham with small-engined AEC 'Regent' V 159 JHX, which was specifically built for use in the city. It paid three visits to the Corporation and even had the gearbox changed from a normal clutch-operated one to a semi-automatic epicyclic unit in an attempt to win a contract. It had virtually a standard destination box layout, and presumably ACV must have got quite close to obtaining a positive result from this vehicle's two months in Birmingham. 159 JHX is in Corporation Street and is about to turn around the subterranean toilets on the left and into Old Square to stop outside the rear of Lewis's department store by the Minories. On the right, behind the Vauxhall Velox EIP, is the Kings Hall Market Hall; it opened in 1907 as a music hall, but became Birmingham's first cinema as early as 1910. *R. Knibbs*

SDU 711
Daimler CVG6; Gardner
6LW 8.4-litre engine;
Willowbrook H37/29R(D)
body; b ?.1955

This bus was built for the 1955 Scottish Commercial Show and had a Willowbrook body built directly on to the chassis without an underframe. The result was a body with an overall height of only 14 feet, but retaining a 'highbridge' layout. It was fitted with a Twiflex centrifugal clutch instead of a fluid flywheel. Demonstrated to BCT between 23 January and 20 February 1957, it was sold to S. Ledgard, Armley, Leeds, in April 1960.

SDU 711

Standing at the City terminus in Old Square, low-height 27-foot-long Willowbrook-bodied demonstrator SDU 711 is working on the 14F shortworking to Mackadown Lane. The Twiflex centrifugal clutch gave a conventional friction drive but with an automatic engagement, thus giving better fuel economy than a bus with a fluid flywheel. The four-bay 66-seater body was fitted directly on to the chassis, and the result was a bus with not only a lower height but also noticeably shallower lower saloon panels below the waistrail. It had the characteristic Willowbrook recessed upper saloon front windows containing air ventilators that could be closed from within the bus. Although built with rear entrance doors, they were left open while it operated in Birmingham. *D. Williams*

3228 (9 JML)
Crossley 'Bridgemaster' MB2RA;
AEC AV 470 7.685-litre engine; Crossley
H41/31R body; b 9.1956, w 6.1969

There were five prototype low-height integral 'Bridgemasters' and this was the second Crossley chassisless example to be built at Stockport. It was exhibited in the Demonstrator Park at the 1956 Earl's Court CMS, and was the first 30-foot-long bus to be demonstrated. Only MB2RA 001, Walsall Corporation's 825 (YDH 225), and MB2RA002 (9 JML) were fitted with flat window pans; the next two chassisless 'Bridgemasters', badged as AECs, also had Crossley bodies but with recessed window pans. The last of the five was for Belfast and had a Crossley body finished by Harkness Coachworks. 9 JML was purchased in order to trial a 30-foot-long and 8-foot-wide double-decker, but was only allowed to operate after the platform staff agreed to collect fares only if there were no standing passengers. This trail-blazing agreement presaged the 'no standing rule' on all BCT's subsequently purchased 30-footers. On 5 January 1959 it was fitted with a Simms-Eberspacher turbo-charger, and, on 9 March 1965, the larger AEC AV.590 9.6-litre engine. It was demonstrated to BCT between 13 February and 1 August 1957, when it was purchased by BCT.

3228 (9 JML)
Top When 9 JML first came to Birmingham in February 1957 it was still in the green and white demonstration livery worn in October 1956 in the Demonstrator Park at Earls Court. It was not modified when it arrived to work the 14 route, but had a special blind made up to fit the single-aperture destination box. Here the 'Bridgemaster' is turning back to the St Giles Road terminus at the traffic island at Tile Cross Road in March 1957. It is displaying an 'ON HIRE TO BIRMINGHAM CITY TRANSPORT' sticker in the lower saloon front window, while the legal ownership is displayed on the first nearside panel as 'AEC Ltd, Southall, Midd'x, Miss G. L. Knight, Sec't'. *A. B. Cross*

3228 (9 JML)
Middle When purchased from ACV Sales in August 1957, 9 JML cost the City Transport Department £4,850. It had been fitted with a modified version of Birmingham's standard front destination boxes and painted in BCT livery in the spring of 1957, although the middle blue band was omitted. With its Crossley Coptic Cross badge, it is parked at the Tile Cross terminus not long after being given the fleet number 3228 on 1 November 1957. It had independent suspension, which gave a very pleasant ride for its 72 passengers, although some conductors complained about feeling seasick! On the other hand, even the fitting of a supercharger in 1959 did little to improve the performance of the small AV 470 engine, although the bus weighed only 7tons 11cwt. *W. S. Godden*

3228 (9 JML)
Bottom The large low Crossley body was an attractive design that somewhat masked the large concealed radiator assembly. The sliding cab door was at first sight a nicely integrated part of the design, though it must have been extremely awkward for the drivers to get in and out of the cab. Several attempts were made to improve ventilation in the upper saloon, with Rotovent ventilators briefly fitted in June 1959, while a permanent alteration was the fitting of opening front windows in the upper saloon. The bus was not very popular with Lea Hall's drivers because, although the four-speed synchromesh gearbox was a typically precise AEC unit, it was harder work than the pre-selector equivalent. Although it was not exactly overworked, it clocked up 204,832 miles in service. Because only Lea Hall garage drivers were passed out to drive it, it was rarely put on routes other than that to Tile Cross. Seeing 9 JML in Bradford Street was therefore fairly unusual; it is working on the complete 28 service from Great Barr to the City Centre terminus in Station Street in 13 August 1966 after receiving the small black waistrail fleet numbers. *M. Collignon*

VKV 99
Daimler CVG6/30; Gardner 6LW 8.4-litre engine; Willowbrook H41/33R body; b 1957

This was the second Daimler CVG6/30 to be built, with chassis number 30001; together with the third, which became Walsall Corporation's 824 (YDH 224), it was the only CVG6/30 to have a Birmingham-style 'New Look' concealed radiator. It had an 18ft 6in wheelbase and the chassis received a low-height Willowbrook body that was a 30-foot-long version of SDU 711. In 1958 it was re-engined with a Gardner 6LX 10.45-litre unit, then was demonstrated to BCT between 23 June and 15 July 1958. It was later sold to McGill, Barrhead, in 1961.

VKV 99

Of all the demonstrators that came to Birmingham, this perhaps came nearest to the traditions and requirements of the Transport Department. It was a 30-foot-long and 8-foot-wide open-rear-platform Daimler with pre-selector transmission, 74 seats and, to cap it all, a Birmingham 'New Look' front. However, its Gardner 6LW engine made it slightly underpowered. The attractive Willowbrook 74-seater body had been fitted in April 1957 and was an extended version of the low-build 'highbridge' body first seen on SDU 711; however, they was never the most robust of products, and the translucent roof, which always gave the impression that the builders had run out of materials and stretched a piece of a tent over the middle of the upper saloon ceiling, rather confirmed that fact. VKV 99 stayed for three weeks during the summer of 1958 and, as usual, worked from Lea Hall garage on the 14 group of services. It is leaving Kitts Green on a bright sunny day, working on the 14E route. *L. Mason*

2211 MK
AEC 'Bridgemaster' 2B3RA; AEC AV 590 9.6-litre engine; Park Royal H43/29F body; b ?.1960

This was the first forward-entrance AEC 'Bridgemaster' 2B3RA to be built and was fitted with an extremely ugly metal-framed Park Royal 72-seat body. Demonstrated to BCT between 14 June 1960 and 2 May 1961, it was nearly bought by Birmingham, and in March 1961 was seen carrying the fleet number 3229, suggesting that it was already BCT property. It was sold to G. W. Osborne, Tollesbury, Essex, later that year.

2211 MK

With its paintwork still gleaming from the Park Royal paintshops, 2211 MK speeds down Alum Rock Road on the 14E route in July 1960 at the beginning of what turned out to be an 11-month stay in Birmingham. This was the 67th AEC 'Bridgemaster' to be built and was the first to have a forward entrance. The entrance doors were not next to the front bulkhead but separated from it by a small window. This setting back of the entrance enabled passengers to get to the rear-rising staircase without falling over the protruding flywheel cover. The bus itself was quite good, although it was hampered, as were all 'Bridgemasters', by not having a semi-automatic gearbox as an option. While the AEC manual gearbox was one of the easiest to drive, the bus was still quite hard work. The Park Royal bodywork was basically a prototype for the GON-registered 'Fleetlines', having yellow ceilings and an interior trim that was to become standard after 1963. The only real problem with the bus was that it was just so ugly! *L. Mason*

2211 MK

From the offside the bus's looks were marginally better, but the short yet wide windscreen and acres of cream panelling above it, coupled with the low-set lower saloon windows, did little for the prototype's appearance. It is seen towards the end of its stay in Birmingham, and the rich patina of the paintwork has been dulled by 11 months' hard work. In its last weeks in the city it was seen by several enthusiasts carrying the fleet number 3229, and for the first time in Birmingham the numbers were not in gold leaf but in black; alas, no photographs of it in this condition have ever been seen. It is standing at the terminus of the 14E route at Lea Village in Kitts Green Road. *S. N. J. White*

8072 DA
Guy 'Wulfrunian' FDW; Gardner 6LX
10.45-litre engine; Roe H41/31F body;
b 6.1960

The 'Wulfrunian' was the revolutionary bus that Guy Motors produced as its high-capacity answer to the rear-engined Leyland 'Atlantean' and the Daimler 'Fleetline'. It was a front-engine, front-entrance double-decker with all-round independent air suspension and disc brakes, but, despite having two demonstrators, the chassis had received insufficient development work, resulting in severe operational difficulties with the suspension, brakes and steering. The latter was not power-assisted, and with the heavy Gardner 6LX engine overhanging the front axle and a full load, drivers had to have almost Herculean strength to turn it. When 8072 DA, numbered thus because of its 72 seats, was demonstrated to BCT between 8 and 16 July 1960, these problems were probably thought to be just on the prototype, but if anything the difficulties got worse, and the cost of development work effectively bankrupted Guy Motors, which was bought by

Daimler. 8072 DA was exhibited at the 1960 CMS and after several years as a demonstrator was eventually sold to West Riding Automobile, Wakefield, for spares in May 1965.

8072 DA

This was the second 'Wulfrunian' to be built from a production run of only 137. Picking up passengers in Burney Lane, Stechford, it is wearing its old gold and black livery with pride – the colours of Wolverhampton Wanderers FC – while working on the 14 service, travelling into the city. The heavily loaded bus travelling towards Tile Cross is 1614 (GOE 614), a Daimler CVG6 of 1948. The independent front suspension pulled the front wheels inwards either when under load, as in this case, or if the large rubber air units became deflated due to a fault. The result was the 'toe-in' look of the front wheels, which increasingly meant that the steering became impossibly heavy. The 'Wulfrunian' was a design that was just one step too far, and it would be another 25 years before a similar layout was tried again on the Volvo 'Ailsa' B55. *A. Yates*

3230 (460 MTE)
Leyland 'Atlantean'
PDR1/1; Leyland 0.600
9.8-litre engine; MCCW
H39/32F body; b 2.1960,
w 3.1978

This was the fourth 'Atlantean' PDR1.1 to be built and was quickly converted to have the bigger Leyland 0.680 'Power Plus' 11.1-litre engine. This revolutionary design, with its transversely rear-mounted engine, Pneumocyclic gearbox and entrance in front of the front axle, made the front-engined 30-foot double-decker obsolete at a stroke. It had a generously low

seating capacity of only 71, but at the end of its BCT career it became a 76-seater. One of the few concessions to Birmingham's specification was the fitting of the standard front destination box layout. It was demonstrated to BCT between 21 September 1960 and 1 May 1961, when it was purchased and given the fleet number 3230.

3230 (460 MTE)

Top Picking up passengers at the Lea Village bus shelter, 460 MTE is working on the 14 route towards the City Centre. The 'Atlantean' is in full BCT livery with crests, and the only clue to the fact that it is a demonstrator is the small notice at the top of the nearside windscreen. The drivers for all Lea Hall garage's demonstrators were specially chosen, but even they had difficulty with gear changes as they could not hear the engine from the cab. The result was that quite often the gear changes were poor, which in turn threw passengers about and made their first impressions increasingly unfavourable. Where were the comfortable moquette seating, the wooden interior trim and the special Birmingham features that had given every bus a distinctive appearance? Instead the new 'Atlantean' was an

'off-the-shelf' job and, although it had the bright yellow and pale blue pastel interior pioneered on 2211 MK (seen in the distance and already looking obsolete), it took a long time for this style of bus to gain acceptance by the people that mattered – the passengers! Not the least of their problems was to find the entrance, and it took a number of years before passengers stopped walking to board at an imagined door at the rear. *S. N. J. White*

3230 (460 MTE)

Above While still on loan, 460 MTE was transferred to Rosebery Street garage and tried out on the 95 service to Ladywood. Still some weeks away from becoming 3230, it is overtaking a parked Austin A35 van in the pouring rain while splashing along Bath Row towards Five Ways with the famous Accident Hospital in the background and Bishopsgate Street on the left. Looking through the steamed-up windows, it appears to be carrying a reasonable number of passengers. This prototype had only two features to really distinguish it from the 3231-3240 batch of 'Atlanteans': the front 'Atlantean' badge and a strangely radiused pair of side windows in the rear dome. *R. F. Mack*

7000 HP
Daimler 'Fleetline' RE30; Daimler CD6 8.6-litre engine; Weymann H39/33F body; b 9.1960

Surely one of the most significant buses ever built, the very first 'Fleetline', 7000 HP, chassis number 60000, was built by Transport Vehicles (Daimler) as a direct competitor to the Leyland 'Atlantean'. With its transversely mounted rear engine, it had the advantage over its apparently similar Lancashire rival in that it had a drop-centre back axle, which meant that its overall height was reduced by about 6 inches and it could have a central gangway in both saloons, something that was not possible with the low-height-bodied versions of the 'Atlantean'. It had a Daimatic epicyclic gearbox, as used on the CVG6/30. It was exhibited at the 1960 CMS in full BCT livery, then demonstrated to BCT between 9 December 1960 and 31 January 1961; shortly after its arrival at Lea Hall garage a larger Gardner 6LX 10.45-litre engine was

fitted. The apparent intention had been to allocate the registration 3229 VP, inferring that it too would receive the fleet number 3229, but Daimlers required the bus for an energetic sales push around the country and 7000 HP remained a demonstrator, albeit latterly with a Cummins V6-200 9.63-litre engine, until 1966. It was then sold to Tailby & George, Willington, and was destroyed in a garage fire on 5 January 1976.

7000 HP
Driving a flat-fronted vehicle along Corporation Street must have brought back memories of doing the same with a Nechells trolleybuses, as the driver had stopped in the middle of the road to pick up passengers! They will have to negotiate what has become a really high front entrance step from the roadway. On 14 January 1961 7000 HP is alongside the shops built into the Central Fire Station, working the 14E service to Kitts Green. BCT was the first to have this very special bus on trial as a demonstrator, and

the fitting of the Gardner 6LX engine made an enormous difference to its performance, as well as making it considerably more economical to operate than the 'Atlantean'. A quick comparison between the bodies of 460 MTE and 7000 HP reveals just how much lower the 'Fleetline' was, a distinct plus point as far as operations in Birmingham were concerned because of the number of low bridges on arterial routes out of the city. It has always been rumoured that because of Birmingham's willingness to allow Daimler to have 7000 HP back as a demonstrator, the pre-production batch of ten, 3241-3250, were purchased on extremely favourable terms! *B. W. Ware*

3231-3240 (231-240 DOC)
Leyland 'Atlantean' PDR1/1; Leyland 0.680 11.1-litre engine; MCCW H39/33F body; es 11.1961, w 3.1977-5.1977

These ten 30-foot-long double-decker buses were delivered with the Leyland 0.680 'Power Plus' 11.1-litre engine mounted transversely across the rear of the chassis. After extensive testing of various demonstrators, the Department had concluded that the ideal bus for future operations would be a front-entrance 72-seater with driver-operated doors and saloon heating and ventilation systems. The demonstrators 'Fleetline' 460 MTE and 'Atlantean' 7000 HP were the precursors to ten of each type of chassis, and 3231-3240 was the trial batch of the latter. They had a Pneumocyclic gearbox, an entrance in front of the front axle, and a generously low seating capacity of only 72, which was the maximum that the

unions would allow; during 1969 all were converted to H43/33F. Weighing 8tons 9cwt 3qtrs, they were exactly 1cwt lighter than 3230, and unlike 3230 the bodies had square rear domes and square side dome windows. The new interior trim of blue and yellow plastics was continued as standard until the end of BCT orders. These were the last Birmingham buses to have tungsten light bulbs and retained the standard front destination box layout with the addition of a small 'TO/FROM CITY' box. The large gap between the thin blue livery band and the bottom of the destination box was the main distinguishing feature between the prototype 'Atlanteans' and 'Fleetlines'.

3239 (239 DOC)
Opposite above Climbing Kingston Hill, Coventry Road, 3239 (239 DOC) has just passed the bus stop outside J. & W. Mitchell's large Victorian paper mill. To the right is a

row of 1930s maisonettes, set back from the road in order that future dualling of Coventry Road could take place. This 'Atlantean' is travelling out of Birmingham on the 17J service to Garretts Green Lane. The helpful display of 'FROM CITY' is correctly set; bus stops in Birmingham had 'TO CITY' or 'FROM CITY' on them as the bus destination boxes only displayed the outer destination or terminus. In order to obviate the usual criticisms that passengers from outside the city did not know in which direction the buses were going, these new buses had this extra display. *R. H. G. Simpson*

3240 (240 DOC)

Below After the successful demonstration of 460 MTE on the 96 Lodge Road service, the 'pre-production' Leyland

'Atlanteans' were used when new to convert that somewhat short route to Winson Green to large-capacity double-decker operation. The 96 unloaded its passengers outside the beautiful art nouveau-style Birmingham Arts & Crafts building in Margaret Street before running around empty to the pick-up point in Congreve Street opposite the offices of the Transport Department. 3240 (240 DOC) is empty except for the conductress, who is standing alongside the driver. It has just passed beneath the bridge in Edmund Street that connects the City Museum & Art Gallery of 1885 to the Council House Extension, begun in 1912. The rear 'bustle' on the 'Atlantean' could always be identified by having three 'flutes' around the bottom of the engine cover as opposed to the two on a 'Fleetline'. *Author's collection*

4.
1963-1969
THE 'FLEETLINE' YEARS,
AND THE END

The deliveries of the production batches of Park Royal and Metro-Cammell-bodied Daimler 'Fleetlines' began in July 1963 when the first of the GON-registered buses began to arrive. This order for 300 Daimler 'Fleetline' CRG6LXs was the largest ever made by any operator other than London Transport. The author remembers seeing 3257 and others standing in a line in Coventry Road garage and at once feeling both excitement at these factory-fresh-smelling buses and yet a disappointment that they lacked any interior wood trim or anything that gave them 'that Birmingham look'. But this was 1963 and bright yellow plastic ceilings and blue Formica was the order of the day. Single-skinned front and rear domes added to the feeling that these bodies were cheap and cheerful, yet they were 72-seaters with electrically operated front doors and fluorescent strip saloon lighting. In addition they had specially designed curved, rather than box-shaped, staircases that were a distinct improvement on those fitted to the prototype 'Atlanteans' and 'Fleetlines'. The buses had a new side-by-side destination box layout as well as having the 'TO CITY/FROM CITY' destination display.

With monotonous regularity a new batch of Daimler 'Fleetlines', 50 bodied by Park Royal and 50 by Metro-Cammell, arrived with C registrations beginning KOV and BON, completing the first large order. The Park Royal vehicles retained their flat fronts and recessed windscreens, so that by the time of the 1965 deliveries they were beginning to look extremely dated. On the other hand the last ten of the 1964 KOV-registered batch of Metro-Cammell-bodied buses, 3391-3400, did have larger, more modern windscreens of either a V-shaped or curved-edged profile, which had been developed for Manchester Corporation earlier the same year and improved their appearance considerably.

Gradually, as more large-capacity buses became available, so routes were converted to Daimler 'Fleetlines', which in turn meant that frequencies could be reduced. Eventually whole garages were converted to 'Fleetline' operation, and by 1969 older half-cab buses were beginning to take a secondary role. On 1 December 1963 the new single-deck 4 service was instigated, serving as a feeder route from Pool Farm Estate to Cotteridge by way of Kings Norton. More significantly, the new service was the first to be operated by One-Man vehicles since the Guy 'Conquest' Cs of 1929 and 1930. Initially it was thought that the only suitable buses were the five 13-year-old Leyland 'Olympic' HR40s, which were the only underfloor-engined buses in the fleet. Three of them were subsequently equipped with ticket machines for One Man Operation on the 4 route.

Meanwhile, the opening up of single-deck-operated routes caused a shortage of buses, so the early delivery of the first 24 from the next new order for 300 Daimler 'Fleetlines' was requested. These buses, 3451-3474, received Marshall B37F bodies and were the first and only single-decker CRG6s ever built, having the advantage of being a standard type within the fleet and also having a single-step platform. There were still not enough One-Man single-deckers, so in February 1966, at great expense, 2252 (JOJ 252), a 16-year-old Weymann-bodied Leyland 'Tiger' PS2/1, was converted with the removal of part of the front bulkhead, the fitting of a swivelling seat for the driver, the fitting of 'Fleetline'-style pastel blue and red trimmed seats, and a Formica ceiling. A further nine of these half-cab single-deckers were converted, but a much simpler method was employed for these buses. The lack of adequate numbers of single-decker buses was due to the proliferation of feeder bus routes brought about by the success of the Pool Farm experiment.

On 9 May 1965 a new service numbered 20 was begun between Northfield and Shenley Lane, then on 31 October the 35 service from Kings Heath to Brandwood Road serving the Allen's Cross Estate was instigated. Further new single-deck services were introduced as the new housing estates at the edge of the city were developed. On 27 February 1966, yet again using the aged Leyland 'Olympics', the 57 from Washwood Heath to the newly built Castle Vale housing estate was introduced and was soon followed on 11 September 1967 by the 26 route from Alum Rock Road to the Bromford Bridge Estate, built on the site of the century-old Birmingham Racecourse.

Meanwhile the second order for the balance of Daimler 'Fleetline' CRG6s was placed in service in 1966, with the first 76 buses registered in either the FOC – D or JOB – E series. The order again was split between Metro-Cammell and Park Royal, with the latter adopting the V-shaped windscreen and a revised upper saloon window design. The 1967 batch was again split on a 50/50 basis between the two bodybuilders, and the vehicles were registered KOX – F and were the final 'Fleetlines' to have a single door.

Further experiments with single-deck buses took place at the end of 1965 and the beginning of 1966 in an attempt to reduce overheads, and, by way of a change in local government, new policies were introduced to alter the running costs and to some extent the image of the city's Transport Department. A lightweight front-engined Bedford VAM5, FXE 892C, was tried out on both the 4 and the 20 route, and with its Strachan 'Pacesaver' body it eventually resulted in an order for 12 Strachan-bodied Ford R192s, numbered 3651-3662, which were introduced on 3 April 1967 on the new Limited Stop 99 service along Bristol Road to Rubery. Although they had lightweight bodies and weighed only 5tons 13cwt 1qtr, they proved to be surprisingly durable as they saw out a ten-year life on a wide range of services, including the later 98 Limited Stop service to Kingstanding introduced on April Fool's Day 1968.

In addition, four rear-engined vehicles were operated on the short 20 service: HWU 641C, one of the first Eastern Coachworks-bodied Bristol RELL6Gs to be demonstrated outside the nationalised BTC Group; CVC 124C, a Daimler 'Roadliner' with a Marshall body; and two Willowbrook-bodied buses, an AEC 'Swift' MP2R registered FGW 498C, and STB 957C, a Leyland 'Panther' PSUR1/1R bodied in Loughborough. There was a move within the large urban operators in the UK at this time to purchase maximum-capacity single-deckers with a large proportion of the passengers standing as 'strap hangers'. Coupled to the idea that certain routes had very high passenger numbers in the peak hours but very low passenger riderships at all other times, the low-seating, 'crush loading' capacity of a single-deck bus with a single-step entrance and a large flat area for the short-haul passengers was thought to be the answer. The new generation of rear-engined single-deckers therefore began to look inviting. In the interim period, the 46 route was introduced on 15 January 1967 and was the first route from the City Centre to be operated by OMO single-deckers. It ran via Hockley and beyond Perry Barr along Aldridge Road to the Aldridge boundary at Queslett Road, placing even more strain on the small, but about to expand, single-deck fleet.

Although not the first choice for the new generation of rear-engined single-deckers, the AEC 'Swift' option was ordered and they were allocated to Acocks Green garage, where they were put to work initially on the 36 service. Fourteen were 33-foot-long MP2R 'Swifts' numbered 3661-3674, and six were 36-foot-long 2P2R 'Swifts', 3675-3680, all bodied by Metro-Cammell with a body style that looked as if it had been using components from the double-decker parts bin! These were delivered in September and October 1967, which by way of a coincidence was the last time an exposed-radiator Crossley ran in service, again with matching KOX registrations. Meanwhile the Leyland 'Tiger' PS2/1 kept soldiering on!

Changes in employment law meant that the five-day 40-hour week made working 'on the buses' a reasonably secure job, although the wages being paid by the local mass-producers of cars in the city made bus-worker's pay look very ordinary, and the intended recruitment of staff never really happened. In a further attempt to reduce operating costs, the Corporation began to introduce OMO double-deckers beginning on 16 July 1967 with the conversion of the 96 Lodge Road service, making it the first conversion in the UK, by which time all the single-deck operated routes were also OMO. The 2 route became an OMO double-decker service on 6 October of the same year, while during 1968 the policy of converting shorter bus routes continued with the 43 service to Nechells, the 95 route to Ladywood and the 39 service to Witton. Other new initiatives were the City Tours, originally introduced for the benefit of foreign football fans coming to the 1966 World Cup games being held at Villa Park, while in 1968 a Christmas Shoppers' Special introduced the Park and Ride concept to a reluctant city population. Other tidying up occurred when, on 27 August 1967, re-booking ended at the Hawthorns, on the cross-boundary services to West Bromwich, Dudley and Wednesbury jointly operated with West Bromwich Corporation, then on 2 June 1968 the prefix 'B' was dropped on the BMMO jointly operated Bearwood, Smethwick, Oldbury and Dudley services.

In July 1966 Harold Wilson's Labour Government produced a White Paper setting out its proposals for the future integration, management and financing of the public transport industry. From these proposals came a further White Paper that proposed the setting up of Passenger Transport Authorities (PTAs), initially in four conurbations, these being the West Midlands, South East Lancashire, Merseyside and the North East, which would link Tyneside and Wearside. The second White Paper examined the possibilities of integrating bus and rail services within these four conurbations, involving the absorption of municipal bus operation into an independent operating group. Company operation within the conurbations would not be affected,

although this was soon seen to be impractical. In the West Midlands these proposals would see the new operating Executive taking over the municipal bus operations in Birmingham, Walsall, West Bromwich and Wolverhampton, although the municipal operation in Coventry was not included at this stage.

In April 1968 the Ministry of Transport informed those areas to be 'targeted' that PTAs were to be set up, while on 29 October the Transport Act 1968 received the Royal Assent. After that events moved quickly. On 1 April 1969 the four PTAs were set up, with F. J. Lloyd appointed as Director General of the PTA at the beginning of the year. The rest of the Executive Management was appointed, while all the four General Managers of the about to be absorbed municipalities were given senior posts in the new West Midlands PTE. Birmingham's General Manager, W. G. Copestake, was appointed as the new Director of Operations, while his Deputy, C. Nurse, was the new Operations Manager for the PTE's South Division, which was the Birmingham City Transport area.

During 1968 the last 100 Daimler 'Fleetlines' originally ordered in 1965 by Birmingham had a difficult start even before they were built. They were intended again to be split between MCCW and Park Royal, but problems at Southall culminated in a drawing being produced in a national trade paper of a two-door-bodied bus for Birmingham City Transport that had a square-shaped rear dome, not the curved Park Royal version. Yet after further problems, the whole batch of 100 was built by Park Royal. They were numbered 3781-3880 with matching NOV – G registrations, and immediately problems with their central doors occurred, culminating in a fatality in Bristol Road South, Northfield, in February 1969. This resulted in all these two-doored buses being fitted with a safety lock in the gearbox, which prevented the bus being driven off with the middle doors open.

The final BCT bus order was to be for 100 33-foot-long two-door Daimler 'Fleetlines' built to the new Bus Grant Standards. These 80-seaters were intended for use on the Inner Circle 8 service, but were deemed to be too tall to pass beneath the two railway bridges on the route, which were each 'plated' at 14ft 3in. As a result, immediately before the end of BCT operation the decision was made to operate them from Yardley Wood, Selly Oak and Acocks Green garages. They were christened 'Jumbos' and the first arrived at Yardley Wood some two weeks before the PTE take over on 1 October 1969, and in variations of the Birmingham livery at least three were used for driver familiarisation in the intervening fortnight. 3904-3966 were eventually allocated to Selly Oak by January 1970 in order to operate the Bristol Road services. Unfortunately the operating conditions were so severe on these services that the Park Royal bodies began to show severe weaknesses after only eight years of use and all were disposed of well before the end of their proposed life expectancy.

The West Midlands PTE took over operations with a new livery of Oxford blue and cream and a new WM logo. The Executive inherited from BCT a splendidly maintained fleet of vehicles, 14 garages, Tyburn Road Works and, in many ways, methods of operation that were as progressive as anywhere else in the country, but with a style of management, processes and procedure that went back to municipal tramway days. The very mixed fleet of buses included 610 rear-engined Daimler 'Fleetlines', which was at the time the largest number of the type in the country. In addition there were 648 'New Look'-front Daimler CVD6s, CVG6s and Guy 'Arab' IVs, one exposed-radiator Leyland 'Titan' PD2/1, two 'New Look'-front Crossley DD42/6s, the surviving nine of the original 30 Weymann-bodied Leyland 'Tigers', 11 Leyland 'Atlantean' PDR1/1s, 12 lightweight Ford R192s, and 18 AEC 'Swifts'. This made a total of 1,311 operational Birmingham buses taken over by the new WMPTE on 1 October 1969 – a bus fleet on its own.

3241-3250 (241-250 DOC) Daimler 'Fleetline' CRG6LX; Gardner 6LX 10.45-litre engine; MCCW H39/33F body; es 1.1962-7.1962, w 9.1977-5.1980

These ten 'Fleetlines' had Daimler chassis numbers 60004-60013 and were the prototypes tested against the ten 'Atlantean' PDR1/1s. Flat fronted and rather 'boxy' in style, they were the first class to be delivered with fluorescent interior saloon lighting, and the last to be delivered with an opening split driver's windscreen. The overall height of the Metro-Cammell bodies was about 6 inches lower than the similar ones on 3231-3240 because of their drop-centre back axle. The transversely mounted rear-located Gardner 6LX engine was

more economical than the Leyland 0.680 and, coupled with the double-decker's lower height, the 'Fleetline' was considered the better vehicle for use in Birmingham. As a result of the trials, an order was placed for 300 'Fleetlines', which at the time was the largest single order ever placed by an operator other than London Transport. During late 1968 and early 1969 all were converted to H43/33F. 3246 was used by Transport Holdings (Daimler) as a demonstrator to the BET Group during 1962.

3241 (241DOC)

During the trials with the ten pre-production 'Atlanteans' and 'Fleetlines', examples from both batches were used on the 43 service to Nechells, the 95 to Ladywood and the 96 to Lodge Road, all less than 3 miles long and extremely well patronised during the peak periods. In the late spring of 1962, 3241 (241 DOC) unloads its passengers at the bottom of the hill in Nechells Park Road alongside the Nechells Park Hotel. The 'Fleetline', still displaying the original 'Haig in every Home' advertisement on its side, will turn left and run down to the terminus in Cuckoo Road outside the same dingy terraced houses that saw the trolleybuses parked outside them until the premature conversion of the 7 service on 30 September 1940. *Author's collection*

3242 (242 DOC)

Above A sparklingly new 3242 (242 DOC) speeds up the gentle hill in High Street, Bordesley, when working on the 15 route to the Whittington Oval in Yardley. It is alongside the famous 'temporary' Camp Hill flyover, which opened on 15 October 1961 and survived until 1986, some 18 years after its intended demolition date! The bus is about to take the gentle left curve into Coventry Road and stop beneath the stygian gloom of the bridge beneath Bordesley Station. Bordesley's High Street area was one of intensive industry and the large factory behind the City-bound 2481 (JOJ 481), a 'New-Look front' Crossley DD42/6, is Fisher & Ludlow's car body factory; the company had taken it over from Hoskins & Sewell, suppliers of iron bedsteads to hospitals. *L. Mason*

3244 (244 DOC)

Below In 1964, once the demonstration period had been completed, 3241-3250 settled down at Perry Barr garage to work routes such as the fairly short 39 to Witton. 3244 (244 DOC) is on its way into the City Centre in Corporation Street. Behind it is the College of Advanced Technology, which in 1966 would become the new University of Aston. The MCCW bodies on these ten Daimler 'Fleetlines' were built to that firm's own standard outline, but the addition of pull-in saloon windows, the normal BCT front destination box layout and the slightly recessed driver's windscreen all helped to disguise its otherwise austere lines, further helped by the layout of the dark blue and cream livery, which was subtly divided by the thin blue lines and the khaki roof. It was only in later days that the buses became somewhat unloved and shabby, but while in their original ownership these prototypes always looked smart. *Author's collection*

3251-3300 (251-300 GON)
Daimler 'Fleetline'
CRG6LX; Gardner 6LX
10.45-litre engine; Park
Royal H39/33F body;
es 7.1963-11.1963,
w 1.1977-2.1980

The body contract for BCT's initial order for 300 Daimler 'Fleetline' CRG6LX chassis was split between Metro-Cammell, as expected, and Park Royal, somewhat surprisingly, as the latter had last supplied bodies to the Corporation in 1950. The bodies had a new-style destination box layout, which, although retaining separate destination and number boxes, had them mounted alongside each other. The Park Royal bodies could be distinguished from the MCCW ones by their curved rear dome and the flat-bottomed panel beneath the driver's cabside windows. All were reseated to H43/33F during 1967.

3256 (256 GON)

Above On Saturday 15 June 1968 3265 (265 GON) picks up passengers in Nechells Parkway as it works towards the City Centre. The Park Royal bodies on these early buses were an obvious development of those built by Metro-Cammell on the pre-production batch. This five-year-old double-decker is working on the 43 service, a route converted to Sunday OMO as early as 11 June 1967. Behind the bus are the maisonettes of the 1960s Nechells Green Comprehensive Development Area, while in the left distance are the earlier 12-storey blocks of flats in Great Francis Street, officially opened in 1954 by Harold Macmillan. *L. W. Perkins, courtesy of F. A. Wycherley*

3282 (282 GON)

Below The horse trough in front of the Greenway Arms public house in the fork between Cattell Road and Coventry Road was one of the last to be removed from the streets of Birmingham before it was realised that they were historically interesting and worth saving. On 10 July 1966 3282 (282 GON) inches its way towards the awkward junction where it will have to turn right into Coventry Road before passing its home bus garage and begin the descent of Kingston Hill. The Park Royal-bodied Daimler 'Fleetline' is working on the 54 service, which at this time still largely duplicated the former 84 tram route, the latter having the dubious distinction of being the last major tram route extension in the city, on 26 August 1928. Behind the row of Victorian shops in Cattell Road, where Goodman's ladies wear shop is located, is St Andrews, Birmingham City FC's ground. *F. W. York*

3301-3350 (301-350 GON)
Daimler 'Fleetline' CRG6LX; Gardner 6LX 10.45-litre engine; MCCW H39/33F body; es 7.1963-10.1963, w 4.1975-11.1980

These Metro-Cammell bodies had the new side-by-side destination box layout and were the direct descendent of the 3241-3250 batch of pre-production prototypes. They had more vertical rear domes than the Southall-built examples and the front cabside panel was slightly angled upwards towards the front. The vehicles weighed 8tons 12cwt 3qtrs, which surprisingly was 6cwt less than the Park Royal-bodied buses. All 50 were reseated to H43/33F during 1967.

3302 (302 GON)
Below One of the first batch of Metro-Cammell-bodied buses, entering service on 7 July 1963, 3302 (302 GON) was initially allocated to Perry Barr garage to work on the 39 service to Witton. Within a few months it became one of

the first 17 of the class to be allocated to Coventry Road garage in order convert the two 'main-line' Coventry Road routes to 'big bus' operation. With their arrival, together with the last 40 of the Park Royal-bodied GON-registered 'Fleetlines', the entire HOV-registered exposed-radiator Daimler CVD6s were withdrawn or transferred to another garage. 3302 is crossing the Moat Row junction in Digbeth and has just been overtaken by a Vauxhall Victor FB saloon. It is travelling into the City on the 58 service from the old trolleybus turning circle at the Arden Oak public house near the city boundary in Coventry Road. *R. H. G. Simpson*

3310 (310 GON)
Bottom Having come down Albert Street when working on the 53 service, 3310 (310 GON) has travelled the short distance alongside the arboreal haven of Park Street Gardens and is turning left into Fazeley Street towards the industrial heart of Digbeth. In the background an Austin FX3 taxi, with its smoked-glass rear window, travels out of the City Centre towards the distant Duddeston Row. This area around Bartholomew Street was where the last horse tram route in Birmingham, to Nechells, operated until 31 December 1906. The 53 bus service went to Stechford via Fazeley Street, and was later extended to Shirestone Road in Tile Cross Road on 12 November 1967. In these pre-PTE days the huge new overspill estate at Chelmsley Wood was out of bounds to Corporation buses, being across the city boundary in Solihull, so this was as near the edge of the first phase of Chelmsley Wood Estate as the Corporation could go. *Author's collection*

3351-3400 (351-400 KOV) Daimler 'Fleetline' CRG6LX; Gardner 6LX 10.45-litre engine; MCCW H39/33F body; es 6.1964- 4.1965, w 10.1969-12.1980

The first 40 of this batch were identical to the GON-registered buses and were all delivered by August 1964. 3391-3395 had large V-shaped windscreens, while 3396-3398 had large curved windscreens; as a result of this design change to the pattern first developed for Manchester Corporation, they were not delivered until November 1964. 3399 had a large V-shaped windscreen and 3400 had a curved windscreen and both

were equipped with a Compas Heating and Ventilator System. This delayed their entry into service until March or April 1965. All were reseated to H43/33F in 1967 or 1968.

entered service. These KOV-registered Metro-Cammell-bodied Daimler 'Fleetlines' were identical to the previous 3301-3350 class. *L. Mason*

3353 (353 KOV)

Above One of the main aims of having high-capacity rear-engined double-deckers was that for every ten vehicles due for withdrawal, only nine new buses were required. During the summer of 1964 Moseley Road garage received 3351-3384 from the KOV-registered class and these replaced the delightfully refined Daimler CVD6s 1931-1971 during June and July of that year – 'The King is dead, long live the King!' 3353 (353 GON) pulls away from the Maypole terminus of the 50 route in June 1964 leaving behind 1955 (HOV 955), one of the MCCW-bodied Daimler CVD6s waiting to leave on the 48 service to the City via Balsall Heath; the latter would be withdrawn on 30 June 1964, just 25 days after 3353

3391 (391 KOV)

Below Birmingham City Transport had introduced an hourly Night Service on the main roads out of the City Centre on 15 April 1946; the day-time termini were often not used, and it was strange to see a line of buses apparently in the wrong street waiting for the race to start on the hour to leave for the suburbs. 3391 (391 KOV) stands at its City terminus in Bull Street when working to Perry Common on the last NS5 service of the night. This bus entered service on 1 November 1964, three months after the previous flat-fronted bus. The restyled front end had first been seen on Manchester Corporation's 4628 (4629 VM) in March 1964 and transformed the appearance of the previously rather 'boxy' bodies. *M. Collignon*

3396 (396 GON)

Below The first eight of the V-shaped-windscreen and curved-windscreen MCCW-bodied 'Fleetlines' were allocated to Perry Barr garage. On 19 November 1966, the first of the curved-windscreen buses, 3396 (396 KOV), turns off the last remnants of Stafford Street and on to the temporary road that will take it to Dale End; at this time the Masshouse Circus and James Watt Ringway sections of the infamous Inner Ring Road were being constructed. The irony is that after 40 years this part of Birmingham has been laid to waste once more and is having a third totally new road pattern being built to serve the new Eastside

developments. On the left is one of the many temporary car parks that appeared in the late 1960s, with a Standard Ensign, a Vauxhall Victor FB, a Wolseley 1500 and a Ford Zephyr 4 Mk III saloon being visible. *Photofives*

3399 (399 GON)

Bottom Turning into Colmore Row from Colmore Circus in about 1966 is 3399 (399 GON). The last two of these 50 MCCW-bodied buses were late into service because they were experimentally fitted with a Compas Heating and Ventilator System. 3399 was the first of this pair and had actually been delivered to the undertaking before being returned to Metro-Cammell's works at Elmdon for this equipment to be fitted. This postponed their entry into service until March or April 1965. Both 3399 and 3400 could easily be distinguished from the other eight buses with Manchester-style windscreens by their lack of opening front ventilators, a paucity of opening side saloon windows and a pair of large grilles on the back panel between the decks. 3399 had a large V-shaped windscreen that was tinted orange with electric demisting elements, while 3400 had a curved windscreen and originally had no opening windows at all. *R. F. Mack*

3401-3450 (401-450 KOV)
Daimler 'Fleetline' CRG6LX; Gardner 6LX 10.45-litre engine; Park Royal H39/33F body; es 7.1964-11.1964, w 12.1972-2.1981

This was the second batch of 50 Park Royal-bodied Daimler 'Fleetlines' and they were similar to the GON-registered batch of 1963, although at 8tons 17cwt they were 2cwt lighter. 3401-3405 were converted to OMO in 1967, leaving the Corporation to convert all but 3449-3450 to H44/33F before the 1 October 1969 take-over by WMPTE.

3401 (401 KOV)

Top On a miserable-looking day in 1967, 3401 (401 KOV) waits in Kings Road, Tyseley, alongside the Girling brake factory when working on the 36 service to Stechford. This was the first of the city's 'Fleetlines' to be converted to OMO, on 23 May 1967, and is being tried out in service for the first time later that month under the watchful eyes of the two Inspectors. It is displaying the 'PAY AS YOU ENTER, PLEASE TENDER EXACT FARE' notice and one hopes that the passenger on the platform is co-operating with the slightly hassled-looking driver hunched over his newly fitted automatic ticket machine. *L. Mason*

3414 (414 KOV)

Middle For almost three years the new 'Fleetlines' allocated to Acocks Green garage worked alongside exposed-radiator Crossleys. 3414 (414 KOV), one of the second batch of rather plain-styled Park Royal-bodied examples, entered service on 2 August 1964 and is travelling past the Birmingham Co-Operative Society's department store in High Street when leaving the City Centre on the 44 service to Lincoln Road North, Acocks Green. By way of contrast, behind it is 2344 (JOJ 344), a Crossley-bodied Crossley DD42/6, which, although only 14 years older, is from another age. The Daimler has a rear engine, semi-automatic gearbox, front entrance, air brakes, front staircase, heaters, electric doors and fluorescent saloon lighting, none of which the Crossley has, yet despite the criticism often levelled at the Crossley, the steering was lighter than that of the 'Fleetline'! 2344 is running on the 44H service to Acocks Green village and would work alongside the 'Fleetline' for 2½ years being withdrawn on 28 February 1967. *A. B. Cross*

3432 (432 KOV)

Bottom Quinton garage received 21 new Park Royal-bodied Daimler 'Fleetlines' in September 1964, replacing the last of that garage's GOE-registered Daimler CVG6s and some of the short-length Guy 'Arab' IVs. 3432 (432 KOV) accelerates down the steep hill in Harborne Road as it travels away from the bus shelter near the corner of Nursery Road. It is working on the 3 route and has just passed through Harborne, having come from the western outer suburb of Quinton. The 3 service was introduced by BMMO in 1912 and taken over on 4 October 1914, when all Midland Red services within the city were transferred to the Corporation. *R. F. Mack*

3451-3474 (BON 451-474C)
Daimler 'Fleetline' CRG6LX; Gardner 6LX 10.45-litre engine; Marshall B37F body; es 3.1965-9.1965, w 4.1979-4.1981

Twenty-four Daimler 'Fleetline' chassis were ordered for delivery in 1965 to standardise the fleet. They were originally intended to replace the Leyland 'Tiger' PS2/1s, but in fact augmented them for the next four years. These were the first 'Fleetlines' to be bodied as single-deckers and were the only ones to be designated CRG rather than the later SRG. The chassis were numbered 61093-61116 and had the standard 16ft 3in wheelbase, though the bodies were slightly longer at 30ft 6in. The Marshall body had an attractive BET Federation-style windscreen and front apron as well as a

slightly longer platform, but otherwise looked like a standard double-decker lower saloon, even to the extent of having the usual rear-engine 'bustle'; it was perhaps a shame that the 'bustle' was not incorporated into the body as with the slightly later 33-foot-long vehicles. The ramp-floored body had a seating capacity of only 37. The buses were used on all the existing and new single-deck-operated BCT services.

3451 (BON 451C)
Below The 4 route was first operated on 1 December 1963 and ran between Cotteridge, Kings Norton, Parsons Hill, Walkers Heath Road and Pool Farm. As well as being the first OMO route operated by BCT since the normal-control Guy 'Conquest' Cs of 1929 and 1930, the 4 was an extremely hilly route, with the terminus in Sisefield Road at

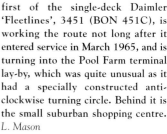

the bottom of Hillmeads Road. The first of the single-deck Daimler 'Fleetlines', 3451 (BON 451C), is working the route not long after it entered service in March 1965, and is turning into the Pool Farm terminal lay-by, which was quite unusual as it had a specially constructed anti-clockwise turning circle. Behind it is the small suburban shopping centre. *L. Mason*

3452 (BON 452C)
Bottom Another new route to be introduced in the 1960s was the OMO 35 service between Kings Heath and Brandwood Park Road. First operated on 31 October 1965, it was seen as a

suburban 'feeder' service as it travelled only 1¼ miles along Vicarage Road, Allens Croft Road and into Brandwood Road. Speeding along Vicarage Road being followed by a Hillman Super Minx estate car is 3452 (BON 452C); it is approaching the Kings Heath terminus in All Saints Road opposite All Saint's Parish Church, which stands on the corner of Vicarage Road and High Street, Kings Heath. On the opposite side of the road is the bus shelter at the Kings Heath stage bus stop for the clockwise Outer Circle route. *R. F. Mack*

3456 (BON 456C)

Above right Perhaps the bus route best associated with the unusual Marshall-bodied single-deck Daimler 'Fleetlines' was the 27. Standing at the bus stop in Church Road, Northfield, in the summer of 1966 is 3456 (BON 456C), not long after the route's conversion to OMO on 19 July. The driver can be seen preparing the ticket machine for the next passenger. One advantage the attracted BCT to these unusual single-deckers was that they had a single-step entrance and a flat saloon floor, which certainly encouraged potential passengers. Behind the bus is the large elevated Bryant site hut, which briefly dominated the corner Bristol Road South and Church Road site while the Grosvenor Shopping Centre was being built. *S. N. J. White*

3472 (BON 472C)

Below The new 57 route was the first bus service into the as yet still unfinished Castle Vale Estate. It was introduced on 27 February 1966 as a feeder service and travelled from the Fox & Goose public house in Washwood Heath Road, where the old 10 tram terminated, via Coleshill Road and Chester Road before turning into Tangmere Drive, the spine road for the housing estate. It did not take too long for many of these short single-deck-operated mid-1960s bus services to cease being feeders to the 'main-road' bus routes to the City and become a more important service or be subsumed within a more useful route. Although the 57 was extended to the shopping centre at Reed Square, passengers wanted a bus service from Castle Vale into the City Centre and on 5 March 1967 the 67 route was introduced via the nearby Tyburn Road, which left the 57 for school journeys only. 3472 (BON 472C) travels along Coleshill Road in the summer of 1966. *Author's collection*

3475-3524 (BON 475-524C)
Daimler 'Fleetline' CRG6LX; Gardner 6LX 10.45-litre engine; Park Royal H39/33F body; es 10.1965-1.1967, w 4.1978-4.1981

This was the final batch of 50 Park Royal-bodied Daimler 'Fleetlines', and they were identical to the GON- and KOV-registered vehicles, although for the first time the side indicators were moved to a new position on the lower blue livery band. The Park Royal bodies were therefore something of a disappointment, with a flat-fronted design that had been left behind by nearly all the other major bodybuilders. All the class were reseated to H43/33F between 1966 and 1968.

3478 (BON 478C)
Above The last 50 of the initial order for 300 Daimler 'Fleetlines' were the BON – C batch delivered very quickly within a four-month period. By this time the flat-fronted Park Royal body was beginning to look distinctly like 'last year's model', which was a pity as they were well constructed. On 9 July 1966 3478 (BON 478C) has just turned from Coventry Road beneath the Camp Hill Flyover at High Street, Bordesley, and accelerates down the slope towards Deritend and Digbeth on the 54 service from the Stuart Road junction on Bordesley Green East. This terminus was advertised on the destination blind as 'STECHFORD', though in reality the Stechford shopping centre was nearly a mile away. *F. W. York*

3509 (BON 509C)
Left Waiting in the yet to be completed Reed Square on the Castle Vale Estate is 3509 (BON 509C), displaying the new standard position for the side direction indicators adopted with these buses. It is 5 March 1967 and the bus is about to inaugurate the City-bound 67 service. The newly installed Bundy Clock is about to be 'pegged' by the Traffic Inspector with the gravitas usually reserved for the laying of a foundation stone! As if to countermand this piece of officialdom, the driver lounges against his signalling windows as he watches the conductor, strangely for March wearing his summer uniform, shepherd the eagerly waiting passengers on to the bus. *L. Mason*

3525-3574 (BON 525-574C)
Daimler 'Fleetline' CRG6LX; Gardner 6LX 10.45-litre engine; MCCW H39/33F body; es 12.1965-3.1966, w 10.1973-4.1982

These 50 buses were effectively the production batch based on numbers 3391-3395, which had the 'Manchester'-design front and V-shaped windscreen. Like the previous class of Park Royal-bodied buses, they had their side direction indicators moved to a new position that bisected the lower blue livery band. All were reseated to H43/33F, and 3525-3555 were converted to OMO between 1967 and 1969. 3531 was burned out on 13 October 1971, and

after being used as a training rig for mechanical apprentices was rebodied with a new Metro-Cammell 30ft 6in-long, 8ft 2½in-wide body, which meant that it overhung the chassis. It duly reappeared in August 1978 as 5531 and surprisingly retained the chassis's original registration, becoming the only post-war BCT bus to be rebodied.

3534 (BON 534C)

Above The 46 service to Queslett Road at the boundary with Aldridge was introduced as an OMO service on 15 January 1967, and although initially operated by single-deckers, it very quickly became necessary to employ double-deckers as passenger numbers increased. The 46 travelled through Birchfield and Perry Barr and, at the old 33A terminus at the Boar's Head, turned into and travelled the length of Aldridge Road. 3534 (BON 534C) is being worked as an OMO vehicle and stands at the 46 route terminus outside Frazer Armstrong's boot and shoe repair shop waiting to return to Colmore Circus in the City Centre. *L. Mason*

3561 (BON 561C)

Below Travelling along Margaret Street, with Great Charles Street in the background, is 3561 (BON 561C). It is passing the Birmingham Education Department's offices within the impressive-looking Council House Extension block designed by Ashley & Newman in an Edwardian Renaissance style and opened, after a long wartime delay, in 1919. This bus entered service on 1 March 1966 and was one of the final 19 of the class allocated to Harborne garage. It is working on the 21 service from the Bangham Pit Estate in Bartley Green, and will turn right into Edmund Street then left into Congreve Street before bursting out into Victoria Square. This manoeuvring from Broad Street into the City Centre 'loop' was necessary because at this time, in about 1968, the old Central Reference Library and the Midland Institute were being demolished and the Easy Row and Chamberlain Square end of Edmund Street was permanently closed. *M. Collignon*

FXE 892C
Bedford VAM5; Bedford 330 5.42-litre engine; Strachan B46F body; b ?.1965

There was a change in the control of Birmingham's Local Government with the new Conservative majority also having power over the Transport Committee. 'New brooms sweeping clean' led to new ideas such as the development of Limited

Stop services and the increasing use of single-deckers. The first of these single-deckers was this Bedford VAM5, which was the only one of the 1965-66 demonstrators to be tried on the 4 service. The lightweight chassis had a forward-mounted Bedford diesel engine, a five-speed synchromesh gearbox and three steps into the saloon. It was demonstrated to BCT between 25 November 1965 and 26 February 1966 by Vauxhall Motors, Luton.

FXE 892C
The bus labours up Hillmeads Road as it leaves the Pool Farm terminus of the 4 route in December 1965, on a route for which it was perhaps not best suited. With a manual gearbox, a small engine and a Pacesaver II body by Strachan, whose later bodies lacked any resemblance to being robust, FXE 892C was tried out because it was a lightweight vehicle, and somewhat perversely led to the City Transport Committee ordering 12 Ford R192s, albeit with Strachan bodywork. FXE 892C was also tried out on the even shorter 20 service between Northfield and Weoley Castle, where it was set against the larger rear-engined demonstrators. *A. D. Broughall*

FGW 498C
AEC 'Swift' MP2R; AEC AH505 8.2-litre engine; Willowbrook B53F body; b ?.1965

This was the first AEC 'Swift' to have the chassis number MP2R.001. It's small engine was mounted at the rear, utilising the same framing and components as the Leyland 'Panther', and

had a four-speed electro-pneumatic Monocontrol semi-automatic gearbox, incorporating a fluid flywheel. The Willowbrook body was that firm's interpretation of the standard BET style, and had a low driving position; a single platform step led into the flat but ramped saloon floor. It was demonstrated to BCT between 22 December 1965 and 2 January 1966 by AEC of Southall and sold to Gelligaer UDC as its 35 in 1967.

FGW 498C
This demonstrator worked over the Christmas and New Year period of 1965, and was painted in a predominantly bright red with the waistrail, window surrounds and flashings in pale cream. It was evaluated on the 20 route between Northfield and Weoley Castle at the same time as the Leyland 'Panther' PSUR1/1R, when a direct comparison of the two was made. Realistically, the 'Swift' and the 'Panther' were the same chassis design but were fitted with different engines and transmissions. It is seen being demonstrated to Crosville Motor Services at Upton-by-Chester early in 1966 on the C40 route from Chester. *E. A. Allison, courtesy of J. Carroll*

HWU 641C
Bristol RELL6G; Gardner 6HLX 10.45-litre engine; ECW B54F body; b ?.1965

Introduced in 1962, the Bristol RE was the first of the 1960s rear-engined chassis to enter production, though until 1965 all chassis were only available to the BTC Group of nationalised bus operators. This ECW body had the original curved windscreen and rounded rear dome, while the chassis came from the early 222 sanction of RE chassis. It was demonstrated to BCT between 9 and 16 January 1966 by Bristol Commercial Vehicles prior to delivery to West Yorkshire Road Car as SRG 15.

HWU 641C

All the rear-engined demonstrators worked on the newly introduced 20 service which traversed Shenley Lane from just outside Northfield to the terminus at Somerford Road. Saturday 15 January 1966 was a miserable day as HWU 641C stands in the turning circle outside the Weoley Castle public house, with Shenley Lane separating the bus from the distant multi-storey flats in Long Nuke Road, seen through the winter mist. This bus was only the 15th Bristol RE purchased by West Yorkshire Road Car, and its arrival in Birmingham, fully painted and with West Yorkshire fleet names, must have been something of a surprise. With its Gardner engine it created a favourable impression, but it was decided to look elsewhere, as Bristol buses still had an unproven track record outside the BTC Group. In view of their subsequent distinguished record of reliability and longevity, Birmingham might have been better advised to have ordered the RELL rather than the vehicles eventually purchased in 1967. *B. W. Ware*

STB 957C
Leyland 'Panther' PSUR1/1R; Leyland 0.600 9.8-litre engine; Willowbrook B53F body; b ?.1965

The rear-engined Leyland 'Panther' PSUR1/1 was introduced in 1964, being initially developed for Leyland's customers in Belgium and the Netherlands. The Willowbrook body was virtually the same as the one fitted to the AEC 'Swift' FGW 498C. It was demonstrated to BCT between 21 January and 1 February 1966 by Leyland Motors, and sold to Gelligaer UDC as its 36 in 1967.

STB 957C

Seen in its demonstration livery of black and white and proudly proclaiming that it is the 'Leyland REAR ENGINED PANTHER', STB 957C is working on the Kincorth Circular service when on hire to Aberdeen Corporation Transport. It met with little success in the Granite City, as in 1968 the Corporation began ordering AEC 'Swifts', eventually amassing 37 of the model! The high floor-line of the Willowbrook-bodied bus is evident when the low driving position is compared to the passengers seated in the saloon. The chassis had a stepped frame, the same as the AEC 'Swift'. In Birmingham it was demonstrated on the short 20 service between Northfield and Somerford Road and was deemed the bus to purchase when high-capacity single-deckers for OMO were required. Unfortunately when a provisional order was made, Leyland Motors could not guarantee to meet the stipulated delivery dates, so the order eventually transpired as the two 1967 contracts for AEC 'Swifts'. *Author's collection*

CVC 124C
Daimler 'Roadliner' SRC6; Cummins V6.200 9.63-litre engine; Marshall B50F body; b ?.1964

This was the third 'Roadliner' chassis to be built, numbered 36002, and the first to be bodied as a bus. The chassis was exhibited at the 1964 CMS and the complete bodied vehicle was shown at the Scottish Motor Show in a red and cream version of Western SMT livery. It was demonstrated to BCT between 8 and 17 February 1966 by Daimler Transport Vehicles, and remained as a demonstrator with Daimler until 1968.

CVC 124C

Of all the single-deck demonstrators tried out by BCT in 1965/66, CVC 124C looked the most attractive both from its appearance and operating points of view. The body with the by then standard BET-style front and rear domes, windscreen and rear windows seemed to sit a little lower than on any of the other rear-engined chassis and consequently had a lower saloon window level. It was the first rear-engined 36-foot chassis to be developed, with a prototype being displayed at the 1962 CMS, but it had a Daimler CD6 engine, which was being phased out, so development work was slowed until a replacement was found. If ever a bus was ruined by its engine, this was the prime example. CVC 124C worked on the 20 service during its nine days in the city, and while stationary at the Northfield terminus it looked splendid. Unfortunately, the short ride up Shenley Lane revealed that the engine sounded like dustbins being banged together, to the passengers it smelled of leaking engine oil, and left behind a lovely blue smoky haze as it clattered along the road. It is seen here crossing Bearwood Road at the Bear Hotel when on hire to Midland Red and working on its 214 service to Brandhall. *A. E. Hall*

3575-3612 (FOC 575-612D)
Daimler 'Fleetline' CRG6LX; Gardner 6LX 10.45-litre engine; MCW H43/33F body; es 9.1966-12.1966, w 9.1980-12.1981

These were the first buses in a new contract for 276 Daimler 'Fleetline' CRG6LXs, and were the first to have a 76-seat capacity from new. They had a revised front apron below the windscreen and a new larger style of fluorescent lighting mouldings. 3608-3611 were equipped with a public address system for use on a City Tour service, which began on 25 April 1967, having been successfully introduced the previous year to coincide with Villa Park being used as one of the football grounds in the English staging of the 1966 World Cup.

3575 (FOC 575D)

Left Heading back to the City Centre, 3575 (FOC 575D) pulls away from the Bundy Clock outside Four Dwellings Boys School, Quinton. This was in the days before this bleak, almost upland terminal point was graced with a bus shelter at the Ridgacre Lane terminus of the 3 route. The 3A service was extended from there to a new terminus at Quinton Road West on 15 January 1961. Unusually, the normal policy of the Transport Department to extend routes into new peripheral housing estates as soon as the first residents moved in was not done in Quinton, as

the school had opened in 1939, while most of the Council-owned houses were not completed until the early 1950s. 3575, delivered two months before the next vehicle in the batch, was operated during the British Week in Lyons between 16 October and 5 December 1966. It was the only one of the batch to have an H41/33F seating layout. *B. W. Ware*

3605 (FOC 605D)

Top Throughout the BCT period, all the rear-engined buses retained their front-wheel decorative nut guard rings, which, like the wheel discs on the 'New Look'-front buses of a decade and a half earlier, maintained

the smartness for which Birmingham was renowned. Although they were perhaps the best looking of the Metro-Cammell-bodied 'Fleetlines', they were not very long-lived, most struggling to see out 15 years of service before going for scrap. 3605 (FOC 605D) is in Great Lister Street at a time when some of the Victorian terraced houses were still standing and, in the case of the shop almost hidden by the bus, still occupied. Soon the bulldozers would level the site to begin the final part of the Nechells Green Redevelopment area, which has itself since been replaced. The bus is working on the 14H service on 5 June 1968; note the trolleybus traction poles still in use along this section of the street, while other remnants of the former Nechells trolleybuses, abandoned in haste in September 1940, are the control box and the finials at the top of the poles. *L. W. Perkins*

3609 (FOC 609D)

Above Bus stops in Birmingham informed intending passengers of the direction their bus was going. Thus in this case, 3609 (FOC 609D) is standing at the 'TO CITY' bus stop in College Road, Perry Common, opposite the College Arms public house. This 'Fleetline' was equipped for OMO in April 1967 to coincide with the re-introduction of the City Tours. Its driver is issuing a ticket from the power-operated TIM machine as he works on the 42 service; this had formerly been part of the Midland Red 107 and 109 routes along College Road to the Beggar's Bush and beyond to Sutton Coldfield. The Transport Committee's desire to have a presence on every arterial road out of the city led to the take-over of the Midland Red company routes along both Walsall and College Roads. However, a shortage of buses meant that 41 of the stored Daimler COG5s were re-certified and allocated in twos and threes around the Corporation's garages. The College Road route was numbered 42 and was taken over on 7 September 1958. The board in the nearside window was a remnant of that take-over, informing passengers that fares are protected on the route as far as the Boar's Head in Aldridge Road. *L. Mason*

3613-3625 (FOC 613D-625D), 3626-3650 (JOB 626-650E)
Daimler 'Fleetline' CRG6LX; Gardner 6LX 10.45-litre engine; Park Royal H43/33F body; es 12.1966-3.1967, w 12.1979-10.1981

At last, the 1966 class of 38 Park Royal-bodied Daimler 'Fleetlines' had a more up-to-date frontal appearance, with the latest style of large V-shaped windscreen and front upper saloon windows of a similar design. They had the revised front apron below the windscreen but retained the old style of interior fluorescent light mouldings. The Park Royal bodies on this half of the 1966 order were, at 8tons 19cwt, some 2½cwt heavier than the MCW order.

3614 (FOC 614D)

Top When the City Tours were introduced for visitors to the matches held at Villa Park during the 1966 World Cup, it transpired that most of the passengers came from the Birmingham area! For several years afterwards the Tours continued, using the newest buses in the fleet for that year. The only modification was that they were fitted with a public address system, so the poor driver could be heard reading from a prepared script as he man-handled the 'Fleetline', on his own without the benefit of a conductor, around the Tour route. Years later Guide Friday would do the same, but the driver stayed silent as a courier read from a script written by someone who had never even visited the City! 3614 (FOC 614D) is loading up with sightseers in Colmore Row opposite the Grand Hotel and alongside St Philip's Cathedral on what appears to be a really miserable-looking day in April 1968. *L. Mason*

3630 (JOB 630E)

Middle The new front-end design of this batch was quite startling – the new-style upper saloon front windows looked as though they had been inspired by the Christopher Dodson bodies ordered in about 1932 by a few of the London 'pirate' bus operators. 3630 (JOB 630E) is in High Street in about 1968 when working on the 52 service from the large Beeches Estate located to the east of Walsall Road. It is passing the Birmingham Co-operative department store on its way to the terminus and reloading point outside the Odeon Cinema in New Street. *Author's collection*

3646 (JOB 646E)

Bottom The driver has just 'pegged' the Bundy Clock at the Eachelhurst Road terminus of the 66 service at Hanson's Bridge Road and is just about re-board before leaving for Whittall Street in the City Centre, at the side of the General Hospital. This terminus at the city boundary with Sutton Coldfield had replaced the old tram terminus at the junction with Chester Road on 11 October 1953, just three months after the abandonment of the 79 tram route. Opposite 3646 is Pype Hayes Park, whose perimeter was used for the construction of prefabs, which, although intended to have a life of only 15 years, look remarkably well preserved when nearly double that life expectation. *L. Mason*

3651-3662 (JOL 651-662E) Ford R192; Ford 5.42-litre engine; Strachan B46F body; es 3.1967-4.1967, w 1.1977-8.1977

These were the first 'lightweight' buses bought by the Corporation for use on the city's proposed network of Limited Stop services. The Ford R192 chassis was a much livelier affair than the Bedford VAM5 demonstrated in 1965, although the Bedfords and the AEC 'Swifts' that followed were ordered by the Transport Committee for specific purposes. The Strachan bodies were the first to be purchased from that bodybuilder since 1944, and although their construction was somewhat flimsy, the undertaking did get a creditable ten years of service from them. Their livery was altered so that only the skirt panels were painted dark blue, and there was a much greater area of cream. They were equipped with non-standard, rather hard red-covered seats.

Works Dining Rooms, opened in 1927 and contained 12 dining rooms, changing rooms for 5,000 employees, a library, a doctor's and dentist's surgery, meeting and youth club rooms and a concert hall whose auditorium could seat 1,050. *L. Mason*

3651 (JOL 651E)

Above Although they were built for the Limited Stop express bus services, these buses were frequently used on ordinary single-deck services such as the 27 route. Loading up outside the original red-brick Cadbury factory buildings is 3651 (JOL 651E), which entered service earlier than the rest of the batch on 20 March 1967 in order to train the drivers at Selly Oak garage on the delights of a Ford gearbox. The disadvantage of the Ford for OMO was that passengers had to negotiate four steps into the saloon as well as the somewhat intrusive black-painted engine cover, which caused a bottleneck at the top of the steps. The driver is issuing tickets from his electrically operated TIM ticket machine, but it is a slow process! Behind the Ford is 2250 (JOJ 250), a Weymann-bodied Leyland 'Tiger' PS2/1, withdrawn at the end of April 1967 just days after the last of the Fords entered service. In the background is the huge

3652 (JOL 652E)

Below The Limited Stop 99 service was introduced on 3 April 1967 and only operated in the morning and evening peak periods. The route covered the normal 63 service between Navigation Street and Rubery, but such was its popularity that buses other than the speedy Fords had to be drafted in. Earlier in this volume a 1950 Leyland 'Tiger' PS2/1 was shown working on the 99 service, and on one occasion a 'New Look' Crossley DD42/6 was pressed into service by an Inspector who urgently needed an extra vehicle – that must have been a somewhat sedate version of an 'express' service! Passing the Limited Stop bus sign for the 99 service in Bristol Road South is 3652 (JOL 652E), travelling through the Northfield shopping area at a time of some major retail development, on its way towards Selly Oak and the City Centre during the first month of the route's operation. *L. Mason*

3661 (JOL 661E)

Exactly a year after the first Limited Stop service was introduced, the 98 route was begun. This went to The

Circle in Kingstanding Road from outside the Odeon cinema in New Street, but went to Perry Barr by way of Snow Hill Ringway, Summer Lane and Alma Street before reaching Six Ways, Aston. As if to prove that it was an express service, it used the underpass at Perry Barr before turning alongside the Alexander Stadium in Aldridge Road. 3661 (JOL 661E) appears to be braking hard in Snow Hill Ringway for a prospective passenger. It is a very miserable day as the modern-looking Ford is overtaken by a short-length Guy 'Arab' III Special working on the 16 route to Hamstead. Now, the question is, did the driver of the bus stop in time for the anxious lady with the headscarf who is half-heartedly hailing it, or did he decide that she was too late? *L. Mason*

3663-3674 (KOX 663-674F)
AEC 'Swift' MP2R; AEC AH505 8.2-litre horizontal engine; MCW B37D+30 body; es 9.1967-10.1967, w 1.1977-9.1977

The first batch of 12 AEC 'Swift' rear-engined chassis were 33-foot-long vehicles and had Metro-Cammell two-door bodies with most of the seating in the rear raised section, leaving the front for supposedly 30 standing passengers who shared this area with a large luggage rack over the nearside wheel arch and a single bench seat for three people over the offside wheel arch. These were the buses ordered as a result of the previous year's demonstrations, and although by no means the preferred

choice, AEC could guarantee a delivery date in time for the conversion of the inter-urban 36 service to single-deck operation. The somewhat unusual bodies looked as if they had been assembled from a double-decker parts bin! At Christmas 1967, three of the buses were used for Shoppers' Specials but the service was poorly used, partly due to the layout of the buses; in later years buses with seats became far more popular on a similar festive service.

3663 (KOX 663F)

Below A Rover 2000 saloon speeds towards Aston Church Road as 3663 (KOX 663F) pulls away from the temporary bus stop in the still cobbled Nechells Park Road not long

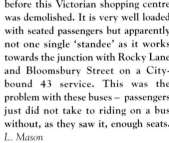

before this Victorian shopping centre was demolished. It is very well loaded with seated passengers but apparently not one single 'standee' as it works towards the junction with Rocky Lane and Bloomsbury Street on a City-bound 43 service. This was the problem with these buses – passengers just did not take to riding on a bus without, as they saw it, enough seats. *L. Mason*

3665 (KOX 665F)

Opposite above With a flat 6d fare for adults and 3d for children, the introduction of a Christmas Shoppers' Special bus service around and through the City Centre on 1 December 1967 must have been seen as both a useful public service and a money-spinner. It operated

Mondays-Saturdays until Saturday 23 December, a total of 18 days. As can be seen from the extensive route board, specially fitted to three buses of this batch, the service was unidirectional but went to virtually every important location inside the Inner Ring Road. 3665 (KOX 665F) and its two-man crew wait in vain for even a solitary passenger as it stands in Colmore Circus alongside the Birmingham Post & Mail Building. *L. Mason*

3666 (KOX 666F)

Below The 'spiritual' home of all the AEC 'Swifts' was the inter-urban 36 service, although very soon it was realised that a 76-seater double-decker could do the job better as no one had to stand. 3666 (KOX 666F) overtakes a parked two-door Morris Minor 1000 saloon in Millhouse Road, Stechford, near to the junction with Wash Lane when working towards the Stuarts Road terminus about half a mile away. This part of the bus route, through Yardley Fields and Stechford, was a large 1920s Council-built housing estate with neat rows of terraced blocks of what were termed either 'parlour' or 'non-parlour' homes with three or even four bedrooms. Yet two

miles away in Tyseley, from where 3666 has recently come, the 36 route's urban landscape could not have been more different as there was not a house in sight, just block after block of industrial developments. *R. F. Mack*

3675-3680 (KOX 675-680F)
AEC 'Swift' 2P2R; AEC AH691 11.3-litre
horizontal engine; MCW B37D+39 body;
es 10.1967, w 7.1977

The second batch of rear-engined AEC 'Swifts' was the 36-foot-long 2P2R option with the larger AH691 11.3-litre engine. The bodies were built to the same specification as the 12 MP2Rs except that in front of the central doorway there was an extra half-length bay supposedly allowing for 39 standing passengers. They were purchased for use on routes where the peak-hour business was very busy while off-peak use was limited, the 36 being the first to be converted. 'Crush loading' single-deckers were becoming something of a national vogue, but within months complaints from passengers used to a seat and not a strap resulted in no more being purchased.

3678 (KOX 678F)
Top Negotiating traffic islands, bollards, pavements and gnarled old trees is not easy with a 36-foot-long bus. If the street furniture was as awkwardly placed as here at the junction of College Road and Springfield Road, the panels of the bus were decidedly at risk unless the driver was extremely careful. 3678 (KOX 678F) has just left Stratford Road and has travelled up the hill in College Road with the driver no doubt planning his manoeuvre around the island and wondering why he had such a long bus that day! *L. Mason*

3679 (KOX 679F)
Middle The driver of 3679 (KOX 679F) has abandoned his driving seat but has left the windscreen wiper on as the bus lies over in St Martin's Circus on an appalling winter's day. The bus is parked next to the Rotunda and about as near as it could get to the entrance to New Street Station, to the right of the bus. The extra half-bay behind the centre door shows that this is one of the 36-foot-long vehicles. These spent most of their BCT lives working from Acocks Green garage, and after 12 November 1967 the 44 service was operated on Sundays by these single-deckers. *ATPH*

3680 (KOX 680F)
Bottom Next to the Cadbury chocolate factory in Bournville is the Worcester & Birmingham Canal aqueduct and an adjacent bridge carrying the former Birmingham Suburban railway over Bournville Lane at Bournville Station. This was an obstacle not really designed for bus operation: on the Cadbury side there was an awkward turn into the long, dark almost tunnel-like length of the combined bridges, guarded by a safety mirror. At the Stirchley end, the road was quite narrow as it passed into an area of late-Victorian terraced housing begun after the opening of Stirchley Street Station, later Bournville Station, in 1876. 3680 (KOX 680F) gingerly negotiates the 10-foot-high bridge when working on the 27 route to Kings Heath. Only recently the standard bus on this route would have been a 27ft 6in by 7ft 6in front-engined, manual-gearbox Leyland 'Tiger' PS2/1, so these 'Swifts' must have been something of a culture shock to Selly Oak garage's more elderly drivers, who had specific single-deck turns that were considered fairly easy for drivers reaching retirement age. *L. Mason*

3681-3730 (KOX 681-730F)
Daimler 'Fleetline' CRG6LX; Gardner 6LX 10.45-litre engine; MCW H43/33F body; es 9.1967-12.1967, w 1.1980-11.1982

Although externally very similar to the 3575-3612 batch of MCW-bodied 'Fleetlines', these 50 buses introduced the two-step entrance to the fleet, enabling the lower saloon floor to be virtually flat throughout. When first delivered, the entire class was allocated to Cotteridge garage.

3689 (KOX 689F)

Top On 12 November 1968 3689 (KOX 689F), working on the 47 service from Groveley Lane, Turves Green, overtakes Park Royal-bodied 'Fleetline' 3735 (KOX 735F). 3689 is travelling over the remains of the long-abandoned tram tracks and cobbles in Navigation Street towards its City terminus, moved on 4 February 1968 from Navigation Street round the corner into John Bright Street. 3735 is standing at the terminus of the 61 route to the Egghill Lane Estate and is three months newer than 3689. Standing side by side, the two bodies provide an interesting comparison with the latest style of front dome windows in the Park Royal vehicle providing a contrast of interpretation by the two bodybuilders for the 1967 contract for 50 bodies each on the Daimler 'Fleetline' chassis. *J. Carroll*

3697 (KOX 697F)

Middle In the days when Pan-Am's aircraft ruled the North Atlantic airways, 3697 (KOX 697F), carrying an advertisement for the US airline, turns from Pershore Road into Belgrave Road, before Belgrave Middleway and its associated underpass were built. Behind it is one of the larger houses in this area, which was known as St Martins; it was always regarded as the better end of Balsall Heath as the 1840s houses had quite large plots of land, whereas within 20 years the heirs of the Edwards family who owned the land gradually squeezed more and more poor-quality houses into smaller plots. The bus is working into the City Centre from Groveley Lane on the 47 service. This was introduced on 2 April 1967 to serve the Longbridge area beyond Turves Green, and operated along Pershore Road alternating with the 41 service to Longbridge Lane, Turves Green, within sight of the former Austin Motor Works at Longbridge, which by this time was owned by the British Leyland Motor Corporation. *R. F. Mack*

3722 (KOX 722F)

Bottom The Metro-Cammell bodies on the KOX batch of 50 buses were to be the last from that company for BCT before the WMPTE take-over on 1 October 1969. 3722 (KOX 722F) entered service on 7 November 1967 from Cotteridge garage and was to stay at the former CBT tram depot for only about 14 months. These pleasantly proportioned buses looked very smart during their brief BCT lives, and this one is no exception. It is working on the 45 service to West Heath and is picking up passengers outside Kings Norton Junior and Infants School in Pershore Road South. *M. Bennett*

3731-3780 (KOX 731-780F)
Daimler 'Fleetline' CRG6LX; Gardner 6LX 10.45-litre engine; Park Royal H43/33F body; es 1.1968-4.1968, w 5.1981-11.1982

Although externally very similar to the 3613-3650 batch of Park Royal-bodied 'Fleetlines', these 50 buses had two-step entrances. They were the last single-door 'Fleetlines' to be delivered to BCT.

3733 (KOX 733F)

Top Speeding into Digbeth from Deritend is 3733 (KOX 733F) from the batch delivered in January 1968. They were virtually the same as the previous batch of 38 and even weighed the same at 8tons 19cwt. 3733 was initially allocated to Coventry Road garage, where these buses replaced the 1951 Daimler CVD6s, which were the original trolleybus replacement vehicles. It is working on the 58 service from the city boundary just beyond the old trolleybus turning circle at Arden Oak Road and is approaching the Midland Red Coach Station and the junction with Rea Street. *R. F. Mack*

3740 (KOX 740F)

Middle The widening of the Horsefair and Bristol Street between the Inner Ring and Middle Ring Roads is well under way as 3740 (KOX 740F) bumps its way over the temporary road service having just passed the junction with Bromsgrove Street. All the buildings on the right survived the redevelopment, while on the opposite side of the road everything was demolished. 3740 is on its way to the Lickey Road terminus at Rednal, a route that had been numbered 62 when it replaced the trams on 5 July 1952. These last single-door 'Fleetlines' always seemed to be somewhat unloved, especially after the PTE took over, and although they were replaced by more modern MCW 'Metrobus' Mk Is, their 13 years in service hardly did justice to them. *R. F. Mack*

3776 (KOX 776F)

Bottom The Stratford Road tram route saw the penultimate extension on the Birmingham system on 2 April 1928 when its terminus reached almost the last yard inside the city boundary with Shirley. When buses took over on 6 January 1937 they had little option but to stop at the same point, as they were not allowed to operate beyond the boundary. In order for them to turn round, a gap was cut in the former tram central reservation, and it is here on 31 March 1968 that 3776 (KOX 776F) waits alongside the green-painted former tram shelters before returning along Stratford Road on the 37 service to the City Centre. *M. R. Keeley*

3781-3880 (NOV 881-880G)
Daimler 'Fleetline' CRG6LX; Gardner 6LX 10.45-litre engine; Park Royal H43/29D body; es 11.1968-5.1969, w 1.1982-11.1983

These were the first two-door buses ordered by BCT and had bodies based on the previous single-door Park Royal-bodied Daimler 'Fleetlines'. The centre door and forward-rising staircase resulted in a loss of four lower saloon seats. A drawing in *Bus & Coach* magazine suggested that they were to be bodied by Metro-Cammell, as it showed a 'Fleetline' with a two-door body and a square rear dome. 3810 was exhibited at the 1968 CMS on the Charles Roe stand, while 3830 went to the British Exhibition, Frankfurt-am-Main, West Germany, from 9 to 14 July 1970. 3867 was converted to O43/22F by WMPTE in October 1978.

3781 (NOV 781G)
Top The 1968 deliveries of these new double-door buses looked at first glance to be very similar to the previous class, but the lower saloon layout with the central staircase coming out opposite the middle exit doors meant that the staircase panel was located amidships on the offside. The first of the class, 3781 (NOV 781G), entered service on 1 November 1968 and is seen here approaching the Nechells terminus of the 43 service when brand new and being used as an OMO bus. These buses were fraught with problems, as drivers had a very limited view of the centre doors and soon began to question the safety of the exit. Unfortunately, within six months of entering service, outside the Traveller's Rest public house in Northfield, an elderly lady passenger got caught in the centre doors and was subsequently dragged to her death. As a result the buses were modified with a time-lag device that prevented a gear from being engaged before the doors were fully closed. To some degree this solved the problem, but the device meant that they became totally unsuited on the route for which they were intended, the intensive Inner Circle 8 service, and eventually they were moved to other work. *L. Mason*

3789 (NOV 789G)
Above The area behind Birmingham's Town Hall was swept away in a scheme that replaced a large block of Victorian municipal buildings with a tunnelled section of roadway with, perched on top of it, the replacement Central Reference Library and a remnant of Chamberlain Square. 3789 (NOV 789G), working on the 96 service to Winson Green, emerges from the meandering temporary roadway and turns from the remains of Chamberlain Square into Ratcliffe Place alongside the Town Hall. The elaborate statue rising from behind the bus was erected in honour of Joseph Chamberlain, who had transformed the fortunes of Birmingham in little more than a decade. The Chamberlain Memorial was erected in 1880 as a remarkable expression of municipal pride in a former Mayor of the Town who was still only 44 when the unveiling took place. *L. Mason*

3835 (NOV 835G)

Selly Oak garage became the home for 3813-3878 prior to the Bristol Road group of routes becoming OMO in July 1969. One of this batch, 3835 (NOV 835G), waits to leave the Rubery terminus of the 63 service in the spring of 1969 before heading back to the City Centre by way of Longbridge, Northfield, Selly Oak and Bournbrook. The crew stand against the wall next to the Bundy Clock in the shadow of the newly built Rubery By-Pass Flyover, behind the photographer. Despite being very new, these buses had only a brief sojourn at Selly Oak before being replaced by the 'Jumbos', nearly all of which were delivered new to WMPTE, while 3835 was transferred to Cotteridge garage. *S. N. J. White*

3860 (NOV 860G)

Having dropped off passengers at the Longbridge Works of British Leyland, the 62 service climbed the hill in Lickey Road towards its terminus in the shadow of the Lickey Hills. With the City of Birmingham boundary sign in the background, 3860 (NOV 860G) approaches the Rednal terminus of the 62 service at a spot where the tree-lined former central reservation ends. More than 27 years earlier tram photographers would have stood here to take photographs of the eight-wheeled bogie tramcars bringing day-trippers to the Lickey Hills. The Daimler 'Fleetline' was one of the buses used to convert the route to OMO, but the dual-door bus is still being operated with a conductor, though the notices of intent to undertake this conversion are in the windows of each saloon. *L. Mason*

3881-3980 (SOE 881-980H)
Daimler 'Fleetline' CRG6LXB/33; Gardner 6LXB 10.45-litre engine; Park Royal H47/33D body; es 15/9.1969-1.1970, w 6.1979-5.1982

These 100 33-foot-long double-deckers were ordered by BCT and had the new square-style bodywork built by Park Royal to the new Government Bus Grant specifications. The seating capacity was 80 and led to them becoming known as 'Jumbos'. Only 3881 and 3882 were delivered with the Birmingham coat of arms and the full BCT livery, while 3883-3895 came in the dark blue colours but without municipal crests. The buses were intended to be used on the 8 Inner Circle service, but their height and length meant that they had very little clearance beneath Icknield Street and Highgate Road bridges. Instead the 'Jumbos' were placed in service at Yardley Wood and Acocks Green garages, while 3904-3966 went to Selly Oak garage for the arduous Bristol Road routes, which eventually literally broke their backs.

3881 (SOE 881H)

The first two at least of these 'Bus Grant' 'Fleetlines' were delivered in full BCT livery and crests about two weeks before the PTE took over operations. 3881 (SOE 881H) speeds away from the Black Horse public house junction on Bristol Road South, Northfield, in Frankley Beeches Road when operating on the 18 route towards Bartley Green during its first week in service. Only careful examination reveals that the bus has a WMPTE legal ownership Fablon sticker low down behind the nearside front wheel. This bus was one of the allocation of the first 23 to Yardley Wood garage, where they would operate on this long suburban route. Buses in this class were delivered in a wide range of liveries, the first 15 boasting BCT blue and cream. 3896 onwards had the new lighter WMPTE Oxford blue, albeit with black lining that had previously been unnoticeable when set against the previous Corporation dark blue. WMPTE inherited the last Birmingham buses as they were delivered, and they were about as modern as any other being delivered in the country. They were the largest ever operated by the PTE, and although they set the standard body style for the undertaking, all new ones were single-doored, only 30ft 9in long and some 4 inches lower, at 14ft 3in. For all their trailblazing components, these buses were not a real success as they were plagued with body defects, with fatal weaknesses around the centre exit where the bodies flexed and eventually failed. Yet for all their faults they were an impressive farewell to new municipally purchased buses in Birmingham. *L. Mason*

ROUTE INDEX

This list shows all Birmingham bus routes in operation during the period covered by this book, 1942-69, and most are illustrated herein. **Bold** entries indicate routes introduced since 1942.

Route	Destination (year) pages
41	City-Pershore Rd-Cotteridge-Turves Green (1957) 123
42	City-Perry Barr-College Rd-New Oscott, taken over from BMMO services 107, 113 (1958) 70, 117
43	TROLLEYBUS REPLACEMENT (ex-7), City-Great Lister St-Bloomsbury St-Nechells (Cuckoo Rd) (1940) 15, 21, 31, 103, 105, 120, 125
(NS44) 44	TRAM REPLACEMENT (ex-44), City-Digbeth-Camp Hill-Stratford Rd- Warwick Rd-Acocks Green (1937)
44A	as 44-Lincoln Rd-Lincoln Rd North-Clay Lane (1939), renumbered 44 (c1964) 41, 73, 83, 109, 122
(NS36) 45	TRAM REPLACEMENT (ex-36), City-Pershore Rd-Cotteridge-Kings Norton-West Heath (1952) 39, 48, 79, 123
46	TRAM REPLACEMENT (ex-18), City-Markets-Camp Hill-Stratford Rd-Hall Green (City boundary) (1937-58)
46	City-Perry Barr-Aldridge Rd-Queslett Rd (1967) 113
47	City-Pershore Rd-Cotteridge-Turves Green (Groveley Lane) (1967) 123
48	TRAM REPLACEMENT (ex-39), City-Balsall Heath-Moseley-Kings Heath-Maypole (1949), extended to Druids Heath (1966) 52, 54, 73, 86
49	TRAM REPLACEMENT (ex-51), City-Markets-Leopold St-Moseley (1949) 87
49B	TRAM REPLACEMENT (ex-40), City-Markets-Leopold St-Moseley-Kings Heath (Peak) (1949)
50	TRAM REPLACEMENT (ex-42), City-Digbeth-Bradford St-Moseley-Kings Heath-Maypole (1949) 54, 107
50B	TRAM REPLACEMENT (ex-42), but only to Alcester Lanes End (1949)
51	TRAM REPLACEMENT (ex-11), City-Fazeley St-Bordesley Green (Belchers Lane) (1948)
(NS119) 51	City-Walsall Rd-Beeches Estate, taken over from BMMO service 119 (1958) 65
52	TRAM REPLACEMENT (ex-12), City-Deritend-Coventry Rd-Bordesley Green (Belchers Lane) (1948)
52	City-Walsall Rd-Scott Arms, taken over from BMMO service 188 (1957) 76, 118
53	TRAM REPLACEMENT (ex-90), City-Fazeley St-Bordesley Green-Stechford (1948), extended to Kitts Green (1966) and Tile Cross (1967) 26, 106
54	TRAM REPLACEMENT (ex-84), City-Deritend-Coventry Rd-Bordesley Green-Stechford (1948) 105, 112
55	City-Saltley-Shard End (1951), extended to Hurst Lane (1953) and Longmeadow Crescent (1963) 76
55B	TRAM REPLACEMENT (ex-8), City-Saltley-Alum Rock-Bucklands End (1950-51) 52
56	TRAM REPLACEMENT (ex-10), City-Saltley-Washwood Heath-Castle Bromwich (1950) 43
57B	TROLLEYBUS REPLACEMENT (ex-93), City-Markets-Coventry Road-Yardley (1951-61) 48
57	Washwood Heath-Castle Vale (1966-67) 111
(NS94A) 58	TROLLEYBUS REPLACEMENT (ex-94), City Digbeth-Coventry Road (City boundary) (1951) 48, 75, 106, 124
59	Intended for trolleybus replacement for Lode Lane route but never used
60	City-Digbeth-Coventry Road-Cranes Park (1951) 49, 53, 75
61	City-Bristol Road-Selly Oak-Northfield-Allens Cross (1952) 123

Route	Destination (year) pages
(NS69) 62	TRAM REPLACEMENT (ex-70), Bristol Road-Selly Oak-Northfield-Longbridge-Rednal (1952) 68, 82, 124, 126
63	TRAM REPLACEMENT (ex-71), Bristol Road-Selly Oak-Northfield-Longbridge-Rubery (1952) 82, 126
(NS2/64)	TRAM REPLACEMENT (ex-2), City-Aston
64	Cross-Gravelly Hill-Erdington (1953) 2
65	TRAM REPLACEMENT (ex-78), City-Aston Cross-Gravelly Hill-Short Heath (1953) 8, 88
(NS79) 66	TRAM REPLACEMENT (ex-79), City-Aston Cross-Gravelly Hill-Tyburn Road (1953), extended to Hansons Bridge Road (1953) 70, 82, 118
67	City-Aston Cross-Gravelly Hill-Castle Vale (1967) 112
68	City-Digbeth-Hobmoor Road-Garretts Green (The Radleys) (1967) 8
69	TRAM REPLACEMENT (ex-24), City-Snow Hill-Constitution Hill-Wheeler St-Lozells (1939) 87
70	TRAM REPLACEMENT (ex-26), City-Snow Hill-Soho Rd-Grove Lane-Oxhill Rd (1939) 56
71	TRAM REPLACEMENT (ex-71), City-Snow Hill-Soho Rd-New Inns
(NS72) 72	TRAM REPLACEMENT (ex-72), as 71-Hawthorns (1939) 57
73	TRAM REPLACEMENT (ex-73), West Bromwich-Carters Green (1939)
74	TRAM REPLACEMENT (ex-74), City-West Bromwich-Carters Green-Great Bridge-Dudley (1939) 59
75	TRAM REPLACEMENT (ex-75), City-West Bromwich-Carters Green-Hill Top-Wednesbury (1939)
76-79	TRAM REPLACEMENT, short working Great Bridge/Dartmouth Square, West Bromwich/Dudley Port/Hill Top (1939)
(NS80) B80	TRAM REPLACEMENT (ex-55), City-Dudley Rd Grove Lane (1939)
B81	TRAM REPLACEMENT (ex-30), City-Dudley Rd-Grove Lane-Cape Hill-Windmill Lane (1939) 60
B82	TRAM REPLACEMENT (ex-29), City-Dudley Rd-Grove Lane-Cape Hill-Bearwood (1939) 60
B83	TRAM REPLACEMENT (ex-31), City-Dudley Rd-Heath St-Soho Station (1939) 77
B84-87	TRAM REPLACEMENT (ex-84, 85, 86, 87), as B81-St Paul's Rd, W Smethwick/Spon Lane/Oldbury/Dudley (usually worked by BMMO) (1939)
90	See 29A (1964)
91	See 29A (1964)
95	TRAM REPLACEMENT (ex-33), City-Five Ways-Icknield Port Road-Ladywood (1947) 59, 97
96	TRAM REPLACEMENT (ex-32), City-Jewellery Quarter-Lodge Road-Winson Green (1947) 99, 125
98	LIMITED STOP City-Six Ways, Aston, Kingstanding (1968) 120
99	LIMITED STOP City-Alum Rock-Kitts Green (1959 only) 78
99	LIMITED STOP City-Bristol Road-Selly Oak-Northfield-Longbridge-Rubery (1967) 62, 119

CITY 27, 31, 37
SPECIAL 13, 20, 22, 24, 28, 29, 118, 127
SERVICE EXTRA 80, 91
FOOTBALL SPECIAL 16, 32, 33, 45, 83
AIRPORT 63